# Step Ahead with Rust

SYSTEMS PROGRAMMING IN RUST

# Step Ahead with Rust

SYSTEMS PROGRAMMING IN RUST

Jonathan Creekmore
James Miller

Armstrong Publications

**Step Ahead with Rust**

Jonathan Creekmore, James Miller

Editor: Thomas Backman
Copyeditor: Jamila Bass
Technical proofreader: Owen Sanchez



Published by:
Armstrong Publications LLC
3500 S DuPont Hwy
Dover, DE 19901
www.armstrong-publications.com

ISBN: 978-0-9993618-0-1
Printed in the United States of America
6 5 4 3 2 1

# About the Authors

**Jonathan Creekmore** has been an embedded systems and security software engineer for the last 16 years. In days past, Jonathan has worked on custom RTOS kernels and device drivers for routers, switches, and IoT sensor nodes, as well as Linux kernel modules. For the last two years, Jonathan has been writing security software utilities in Rust, his new favorite programming language. When not hacking on Rust code, Jonathan enjoys camping with his family and spending time in the mountains.

**James Miller** is a developer involved with the Rust project for over two years and seen a lot of its evolution (and have had a hand in some of it). Most of his involvement has been in improving the compiler output, but he tinkered with most parts at one point or another. James spends a lot of time on the Rust IRC channel helping new users. He has acquired a lot of experience guiding people through the language.

# Acknowledgements

Many people provided help during the production of this book; without their help, it would not be what it is today. Particularly, I would like to thank the many technical reviewers who repeated pored through this work, providing excellent feedback, during its rough state. Thanks to Adolfo Ochagavia, Björn Steinbrink, Christopher Dumas, Corey Richardson, Eduardo Pinho, Evgeniy Dushistov, Jonathan Wilbur, Michael Angstadt, Owen Sanchez, Trevor Alexander, Victor Polevoy, Vittorio Romeo for all of your technical assistance. Additionally, thank you to Owen Sanchez for helping to ensure technical accuracy of the text, to Jamila Bass for further reviewing and correcting the text, and the rest of the team at Armstrong Publications for all of the hard work that it takes to get a book published and brought into the real world.

Further, I would like to thank all of the Rust core developers for all of their labors; without their hard work, my favorite programming language would not exist.

Finally, I would like to thank my family for sticking by me and keeping me going while I struggled to finish the book.

Jonathan Creekmore

# Table of Contents

# Preface

Software is permeating our physical world. For years, processors have been added to consumer products and industrial equipment to enable greater flexibility, lower cost, and advanced features that users are requesting. With the rise of the Internet of Things, more and more of those devices are being connected together through networks. As a software engineer, it is an exciting time to be in the industry due to the challenges of writing all of these advanced features. The greatest challenge is to write secure, fast, and efficient code for these devices while still delivering products on time and for a reasonable cost. Rust provides a path forward to meeting that challenge.

Many programming languages profess to be safe languages; however, those programming languages typically provide safety by using a garbage collector, preventing them from being integrated into small, embedded processors that you find integrated into devices. Rust provides memory safety without a garbage collector by utilizing its advanced type system and sophisticated compiler to statically track memory use and to efficiently use the available memory. This allows Rust to possibly be used in places where, traditionally, the C programming language holds sway: the small, embedded systems that control the devices we use every day, from networking equipment, to smart sensors that observe and communicate with the outside world, even to intelligent systems in your smart cars.

## WHO SHOULD READ THIS BOOK

This book is aimed at developers who want to write safer, more-efficient software than they have in the past.have already had some experience with the Rust programming language, but want to increase their knowledge of the more advanced features of Rust programming. Ideally, readers will already be familiar with programming in general and will have at least skimmed the official Rust documentation in the form of *The Rust Programming Language*, enough to get the basic language syntax and semantics down.

## ROADMAP

This book is split into three parts. Part 1 (chapters 1—5) is an introduction and an overview of the type system:

- Chapter 1 introduces the Rust programming language and gives you a brief history of the development of the language.
- Chapter 2 covers the use of Cargo as a build system and explains how to use it to manage build dependencies for your projects.
- Chapter 3 provides an overview of the Rust type system in general and goes in-depth on Rust traits and generic types.
- Chapter 4 describes how you can use traits to provide standard interfaces to your types and how to provide new functionality to existing types.
- Chapter 5 covers the lifetime concept of variables in Rust, explaining the ownership and borrowing of values and how to use lifetimes to efficiently share data.

Part 2 (chapters 6—9) introduces several real-world programming constructs in Rust:

- Chapter 6 introduces the iterator concept, describes how to effectively use iterators, and explains how to implement iterators on your own types.

- Chapter 7 provides an overview of concurrency in Rust by demonstrating message-passing concurrency and shared-memory concurrency in a type-safe manner.
- Chapter 8 explains several common type-safe idioms found in Rust standard library and shows how you can implement them yourself.
- Chapter 9 shows how Rust provides support for unit, documentation, integration, and performance testing of your code.

Part 3 (chapters 10—13) cover advanced topics in Rust programming:

- Chapter 10 digs into the Rust macro system and shows how to reduce boilerplate code by having the Rust macro system produce it for you.
- Chapter 11 explains how to interact with native system libraries using the foreign function interface and how to provide a native interface to your safe Rust libraries.
- Chapter 12 provides an overview of interior mutability and how to use it selectively defer some safety checks to run-time.
- Chapter 13 introduces the unsafe Rust rules and provides some guidance on when to use unsafe code and how to do so safely.

## SOURCE CODE AND DEVELOPMENT TOOLS

The major source code examples discussed in the book can be found on GitHub at `https://github.com/jcreekmore/programming-rust.git`. All examples in the repository should be buildable using the stable Rust compiler for version 1.15.1 or newer.

The easiest way to get the Rust toolchain installed is to go to `https://www.rustup.rs` and follow the instructions there to install the `rustup` utility. Those instructions will direct you to downloading the `rustup-init` utility that will install `rustup` on your machine for your current user. Once rustup has been installed, you can run:

```
> rustup update 1.15.1
> rustup update nightly # for benchmarking
> rustup default 1.15.1
```

Those three commands will 1) install the Rust 1.15.1 compiler, 2) install the latest Rust nightly compiler, and 3) ensure that the Rust 1.15.1 compiler is the current default.

## MORE INFORMATION

If you would like to learn more about Rust, check out the official Rust book *The Rust Programming Language* at `https://doc.rust-lang.org/book/`. For more in-depth information on unsafe Rust programming, *The Rustonomicon* at `https://doc.rust-lang.org/nomicon/` will give you the advanced details that you are looking for. Finally, *Rust By Example* at `https://rustbyexample.com` contains may examples for specific topics that can be run in the browser.

For library documentation, see the Standard Library API reference at `https://doc.rust-lang.org/std/`. For documentation on crates that are not part of the standard library, see `http://docs.rs` for documentation of crates that are published at `http://crates.io`.

Additionally, Mozilla's IRC network at `irc.mozilla.org` contains several Rust-related channels such as #rust for general Rust-related questions, #rust-beginners for beginner-level Rust questions, and #rust-internals for more in-depth questions around the compiler or standard library.

1

# Introduction & History of Rust

Welcome, Reader, to *Step Ahead with Rust*. Rust is a systems programming language focused on three main goals: safety, speed, and concurrency. While many programming languages manage this, Rust does so without the use of a garbage collector or heavy runtime environment. This makes Rust applicable to areas where few safe languages dare to tread such as embedded systems, device drivers, and operating system development, to name a few. Members of the Rust community have been developing an operating system and driver stack called Redox to work towards a complete, safe, Rust ecosystem for their computers. Additionally, developers have been working to build up Rust support for popular micro-controllers such as the MSP430 and the ARM Cortex M parts in order to enable safe Rust code on modern, embedded system devices. However, Rust does not skimp on the higher-level features to push into these areas. With a sophisticated type system as well as a number of modern conveniences, Rust manages to make systems programming easier, safer and faster.

Safety in Rust refers primarily to memory safety, which means no memory corruption and no use-after-free. The Rust language enforces a style of programming that prevents you from writing code that might produce a buffer overflow or segmentation fault in C or C++. This is quite simple if a garbage collector is used and pointers are hidden away (which is what the majority of "safe" languages have done). Garbage collection comes at a price, though, by introducing a runtime that must be present and periodic delays in execution for collection. Instead, Rust uses sophisticated analysis and lightweight user annotations to statically check that the data is always valid when accessed by the program (see Chapter 5). However, a static check may not always be enough. There are times when it is known that the code being constructed is correct, but the static checks that Rust provides may disagree. That is the nature of static analysis. Fortunately, Rust comes with an escape hatch in the form of unsafe code to allow a relaxation of some of the restrictions (such as the restrictions on using raw pointers and aliasing mutable variables) that Rust normally enforces for safe code (see Chapter 13). With unsafe Rust, the programmer is allowed to access raw pointers, call out to foreign code such as native C code, and access mutable static variables. However, programming with unsafe code can be tricky since the programmer has to manually manage resources that the compiler would normally do, but with the advantage that it can allow you to write code that can be difficult to write within the safe Rust framework.

Rust is fast. By compiling to machine code with robust optimizations, Rust is competitive with the performance of other systems programming languages. The following table illustrates how well Rust performs against other languages in a computer program benchmark shootout. The table shows how Rust performs comparably with C and C++, while beating the performance of Go and Java in every category.

| | **Benchmark Wall-Clock Performance in seconds** | | | | |
|---|---|---|---|---|---|
| | **Rust** | **C** | **C++** | **Go** | **Java** |
| Binary-trees | 4.33 | 2.38 | 2.36 | 34.77 | 11.26 |
| Fannkuch-redux | 10.74 | 8.97 | 10.35 | 15.81 | 13.74 |
| Fasta | 1.48 | 1.33 | 1.48 | 1.98 | 2.13 |
| k-nucleotide | 5.27 | 5.38 | 7.18 | 16.08 | 7.93 |
| mandelbrot | 1.89 | 1.65 | 1.73 | 5.61 | 7.10 |
| n-body | 13.16 | 9.96 | 9.31 | 21.52 | 21.54 |
| pidigits | 1.74 | 1.73 | 1.89 | 2.02 | 3.06 |

| | Benchmark Wall-Clock Performance in seconds | | | | |
|---|---|---|---|---|---|
| | **Rust** | **C** | **C++** | **Go** | **Java** |
| regex-redux | 2.70 | 1.45 | 17.14 | 29.51 | 12.31 |
| reverse-complement | 0.33 | 0.42 | 0.60 | 0.49 | 1.10 |
| spectral-norm | 2.50 | 1.99 | 1.99 | 3.96 | 4.26 |

numbers courtesy http://bechmarksgame.alioth.debian.org

In addition to this, Rust encourages you to code efficiently, making writing fast code easy. Unnecessary memory allocations spread data across the memory address space, making it less likely to fit into the speedy processor cache where it needs to be in order to get high performance out of your programs. Rust's move-by-default semantics force the programmer to decide when to copy data around and therefore lead to increased safe sharing of data through the borrow system, lowering the number of unnecessary memory allocations in your programs. Additionally, the highly-optimized iterators provided by the Rust standard library, combined with closures, allow developers to write code in high-level abstractions that compile down to extremely efficient machine code.

Concurrency is a difficult problem and Rust takes a pragmatic approach to handling it. By leveraging the type system, Rust aims to prevent data races in concurrent code. It does this by using ownership to discourage shared mutable data and types to ensure synchronized access to mutable data that is shared. While not as sophisticated as other languages, Rust manages to eliminate or reduce several issues commonly associated with concurrent programming with little to no overhead (see Chapter 7).

Rust is not a simple language as it is designed for building large systems. It forces you to write robust code which can be unforgiving and overwhelming. With such a vast amount of features, it is easy to get lost and not know how to proceed. As such, this book aims to be a guide for those times. We aim to show you common patterns for structuring Rust code in a way that is both efficient and safe. Additionally, we want to provide details on how and why Rust is structured the way it is.

Rust is not an object-oriented language. If you are used to designing programs in languages like C++, Python, or Java, it can be difficult to try to adapt an object hierarchy to Rust since Rust does not allow data types to inherit member variables or functionality from other data types. To emulate the inheritance of member variables, Rust prefers the encapsulation of fields inside larger data types. There is no direct correlation to inheriting functionality (member functions) in Rust; instead, Rust provides the concept of an interface through its Trait system, allowing differing data types to implement common interfaces through a Trait implementation (Chapter 4). Traits provide for compile-time polymorphism using generic functions similar to C++ templates and Java generics. Traits also provide for run-time polymorphism through trait objects that simulate manipulating an object through a pure virtual class in C++ or an interface in Java.

## HISTORY

Rust 1.0 was released in May 2015, after five years of public development. In June 2010, the earliest version of Rust hit GitHub. Rust was originally a personal project by Mozilla employee Graydon Hoare; however, Mozilla saw the utility in a safe systems programming language and began sponsoring the project. While the first numbered release, 0.1, wouldn't be until the beginning of 2012, Mozilla started working on *Servo* in April 2011! *Servo* is a sister project to Rust — a brand-new browser rendering engine and a driver of many Rust features and improvements. Even from the early days of the Rust language, it has been focused on real-world problems and applications.

Rust has been a self-hosted language since mid-2011, meaning that the Rust compiler, `rustc`, was able to compile itself. Prior to that, another compiler, written in OCaml, was used. Known as `rustboot`, it was fated to be made obsolete, being removed from the Rust repository not long after.

The most notable feature of Rust would not arrive until March 2011, i.e. the region system. Now referred to as lifetimes, the feature was very different than it is now, with a different syntax and somewhat less powerful.

It would take years of work and iteration for Rust's signature feature to become what it is today. It was not until a year later, in March 2013, that the syntax we are all familiar with was implemented.

In April 2012, the first runtime was implemented. Focused on asynchronous I/O and "green threads", this runtime was tightly integrated into the language. While it was an impressive piece of engineering, that runtime was ultimately considered to run counter to Rust's design goals. The complex runtime made it difficult to use Rust in many environments, such as embedded systems and integration with other languages. In October 2014, the runtime was dismantled. And by the end of the following month, the majority of the runtime code was removed, allowing Rust to be used easily in almost any context.

Early Rust had many special built-in pointers. While only raw pointers and references survived until now, there existed two (2) others: shared and unique pointers. Indicated by `@` and `~` sigils respectively, these pointers possessed hard-coded behavior. As the type system evolved over time, they became more and more unnecessary since the type system evolved to a point where they could be defined within the language instead of being a special case of the language. Eventually, shared and unique pointers were removed. The shared pointers were the first to go, being removed in November 2013, while the much more entrenched unique pointers were removed in May 2014. The concepts of shared and unique pointers live on in the form of the `Rc` and `Box` smart pointers in the standard library.

In the lead-up to Rust 1.0, Rust added support for: 1) dynamically sized types, 2) associated types, 3) type constraints using where clauses, 4) the Cargo build system, and 5) the crates package system. With all of those features added, the Rust community stabilized the language and gave the promise of backwards compatibility with the 1.0 version of the language. The community set forth a six-week development model, meaning that a new minor version of Rust is released roughly every 6 weeks. Since the 1.0 version, numerous standard library additions such as the `From` and `Into` traits have landed, as well as minor language features like the `?` operator (syntactic sugar that makes using the `try!` macro easier).

In the near future, we hope to see `TryFrom` and `TryInto` land in the standard library, to provide standard methods of converting between types where there is the possibility of failure. Additionally, we hope to see the `impl Trait` functionality stabilize, which will give Rust developers a way of efficiently returning a generic type from a function without having to allocate memory on the heap.

Rust has changed much in its seven years of development. With heavy input from the community, Rust has added and removed many features that are not mentioned in this brief history. However, what is important is what has not changed — a focus on safety, performance, and concurrency. No matter what, you can be assured that safety, performance, and concurrency will always be at the core of Rust.

2

# Cargo

In the beginning, there was C. To build a C program, you would run the compiler on the source file and it generated an executable. If you had more than one, you could compile the files individually and manually link them together in the right order. When you made changes, you had to remember what files needed to be recompiled. So, the C developers created the Make system to determine what files needed to be recompiled. Then, if you wanted to use a library with C, you downloaded the library, compiled it, and built your code against it. However, when you attempted to ship your project to your buddy, it did not build because they did not have the library that you linked against. So, in C-land, you documented your dependencies in a README file so that others knew which libraries you depended against and they could go grab those dependencies themselves every time they got a new code drop. Hopefully, they carefully checked the README with every drop, just in case you updated anything.

In the early days of Rust, the Rust ecosystem was very much like the early days of C. You were responsible for manually downloading and building the libraries you wanted to use. Also, you had to explicitly call out to the `rustc` compiler on each of your source files, linking them together in the right order. However, this state-of-the-art in dependency management has come a long way from the days of a Makefile and a README describing what to build and how to build it. Other languages, like Python and Go, comprised of package managers that manage the build process and keep track of the project dependencies for developers. So, the Rust community built Cargo.

Cargo is Rust's package manager and the starting point for most Rust projects. This chapter will introduce you to the basic use of Cargo for creating and developing Rust projects. This is only a basic overview of Cargo, though, but it is enough to get you started. There is extensive documentation available at `doc.crates.io`.

## OVERVIEW

The crates system is the Rust community's solution to dependency management for Rust programs. Simply put, a crate is a Rust package. A crate can be an executable program, a library, or some combination of both.

Cargo is a software program that is used to build crates by managing the dependency graph for a project. Every crate is described by a manifest file called ***Cargo.toml***. This manifest file describes how the crate should be built as well as the crate's dependencies. When you build a crate, Cargo reads the manifest file to determine what crates are needed to build the current project and therefore downloads semantically-appropriate versions of those crates from `crates.io` – Rust's standard package repository. Then, Cargo reads their manifest files and determines their dependencies, and so on and so forth. Once all of the dependencies are determined, Cargo stores the selected versions of each crate in a file called the ***Cargo.lock*** file, which is used to keep a record of which versions are used for reproducible builds of packages. Eventually, Cargo has determined every crate that is needed to build up the current package, so Cargo can call out to `rustc` to build up each dependent crate in turn, finally building the root crate (i.e., the package you originally wanted to build). Figure 2-1 shows the relationships between the different components in the Rust build process.

As it appears, the ***Cargo.toml*** manifest file is central to the build process. How can we then generate one of those manifest files and populate it with the information that we need to provide to build up Rust crates of our own?

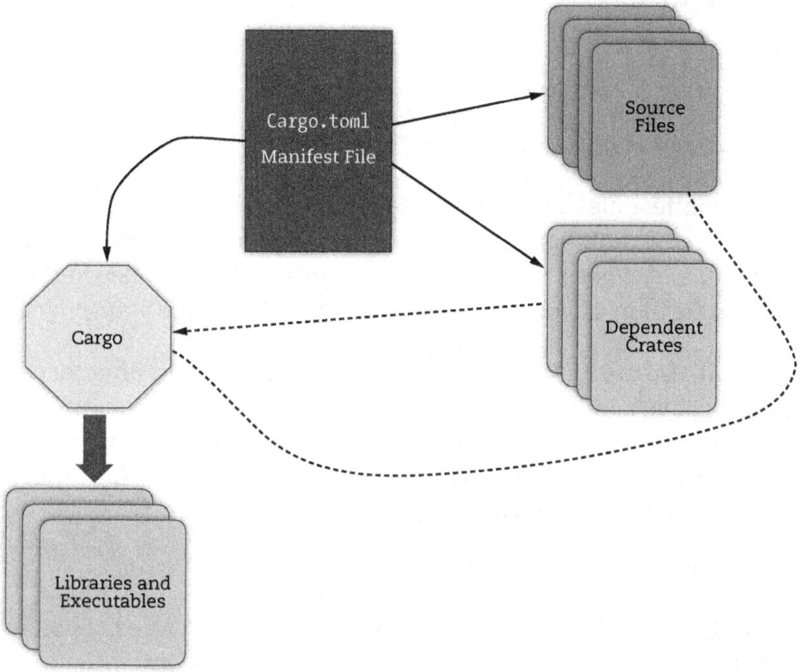


**Figure 2-1:** Relationships between Rust build components

# GENERATING A BASIC MANIFEST FILE

The simplest way to generate a *Cargo.toml* manifest file, and use Cargo to build Rust packages, is to use the `cargo new` command. Call the `cargo new` command with the name of a new crate like this:

```
$ cargo new myproject
```

This will create a new directory called `myproject` and initialize a crate called *myproject* in that directory. Cargo will create a Git repository for the project, add a default *Cargo.toml* manifest file to the directory, and a starting *src/lib.rs* file for the template crate being initialized. So, for the `myproject` crate example, the *Cargo.toml* manifest will look something like this:

```
[package]
name = "myproject"
version = "0.1.0"
authors = ["Rust Devel <devel@example.org>"]

[dependencies]
```

This manifest file names the crate `myproject`, gives it an initial version number, and pulls your author information from your Git configuration. Additionally, it goes ahead and creates an 'empty dependencies' section for you to fill in as you add additional dependencies to your project.

You can also create the new crate inside of the current directory. If you already have a directory called *myproject* that you are in, running the following will create the crate called *myproject* in the current directory, generating the same Git repository and project template files that specifying the directory would create:

```
$ cargo new
```

By default, Cargo uses the library template for new crates. If you want to create an executable instead, you can add the `--bin` option:

```
$ cargo new --bin myprogram
```

In the executable case, the manifest file will look identical to the library manifest file. The difference is in the generated template file provided. For an executable, Cargo will generate a template *src/main.rs* file for you to populate. If you want to create a combination crate that contains both a library and one or more executables, Cargo does not provide any specific template for doing so. Instead, you should simply generate a library crate and then add additional binary build targets to the crate. But what are build targets and how can I add them to my crate?

## BUILD TARGETS

A build target is a final output for the project. There are five (5) different types of build target:

- **Library**
  Library targets produce libraries. A project can have only one library target, if any at all. A library target is what you would typically think of as a crate that is a dependency which can be pulled into another library or an executable. It is not itself an executable program; instead, it provides data structures and functions to an executable.
- **Binary**
  This is an executable that is a main part of the project. You can have multiple binary targets in a project. The binary targets, or executables, are what you would typically think of as programs. Binary targets can be executed by users and are not compiled into other binary targets – they are meant to stand on their own.
- **Example**
  These are example programs demonstrating the use of your project to end users. You can have multiple examples in a project. You would typically provide example targets along with a library target to demonstrate, as well as any documentation on how the library should be used.
- **Test**
  Test programs are those which run when using the `cargo test` command. We will look at test programs in depth later in Chapter 9 but briefly, test programs are used for integration tests between the modules that make up a library or executable. Cargo can interpret the output of these test programs and report whether or not the crate is passing tests based on that output.
- **Benchmark**
  Benchmark programs run when using the `cargo bench` command. We will look at benchmark programs in more depth later in Chapter 9 but briefly, benchmark programs are used to time different function calls that are used in your crate. Cargo will execute the benchmark programs a large number of times and report back to you how quickly each iteration ran (on average).

For each type of build target, Cargo looks in a different place for the entry file when building that target. We have already mentioned where Cargo looks for libraries and executables when we discussed generating template files for crates, but Cargo has other locations it will look at for the other build targets. Starting from the project directory:

```
src/
  lib.rs  # Entry file for library projects
  main.rs # Default entry file for executable projects
  bin/
    *.rs  # Other binary targets
examples/
  *.rs    # Example targets
tests/
  *.rs    # Test targets
benches/
  *.rs    # Benchmark targets
```

Every project requires either a library target or at least one executable or binary target. If you want to add one of these build targets to you crate, simply create a Rust source file in the proper directory in your project tree. The Cargo build process will pick them up when you perform a build. However, we haven't yet seen how to build one of our Rust crates. How do we accomplish this?

## BUILDING YOUR CRATE

To build your crate, you use the command `cargo build`. This command executes the compiler, looking for either a file named ***lib.rs***, for library projects, or ***main.rs***, for executable projects.

By default, Cargo builds in debug mode. This means that no optimizations are done and all the debugging information is generated. You can compile in "release" mode, which enables optimization by adding the `--release` option:

```
$ cargo build --release
```

To build other targets, you can use the `--bin`, `--example`, `--test`, and `--bench` options to build specific binary, example, test and benchmark targets respectively.

```
$ cargo build --bin mybinary
$ cargo build --example myexample
$ cargo build --test mytest
$ cargo build --bench mybench
```

When you build any target, the output is stored in the ***target/{debug,release}/*** directory. Building executables is all well and good, but an executable does not do you any good unless it is run. You can run the executable like:

```
./target/debug/mybinary --prog-arg
```

Or, you could allow Cargo to abstract away the location and specifics of running the executable.

## Running Executables

If you're building a program or an example, just compiling it may not be enough. To run the executable, you can use the `cargo run` command.

```
$ cargo run
```

If the crate has only one binary target, then the debug build of that target will be executed. If you have not already built the program, or if the program source code has been changed since you last built it, Cargo will go ahead and make sure that the program is up-to-date, i.e., it has been built against any changes you might have made in the crate.

If you want to pass arguments to the program, use the following style of command:

```
$ cargo run -- --prog-arg
```

Once again, if the crate only has one binary target, then the debug build of it will be executed. The arguments after the -- are passed along to the executable being run. In this case, the program will be passed the **`--prog-arg`** argument.

Alternatively, if you want to run the release version of the executable, simply pass the **`--release`** flag to the run command as follows:

```
$ cargo run --release -- --prog-arg
```

If you have more than one binary target, or want to run an example, then you can use the **`--bin`** and **`--example`** options to specify the executable just as you would to the build command:

```
$ cargo run --bin other_bin -- --other-arg
```

# GENERATING DOCUMENTATION

Having good documentation to follow is necessary when using someone else's library. While we will give a brief overview on how to document your own crate in Chapter 9, it should be noted that Cargo provides a command that will allow you to generate a local copy of your crate's documentation and every crate it depends on. The crate documentation provides a list of all of the public data structures and functions that are exported by the crate, along with the module layout of the crate. This allows you to see what types and parameters are needed to call functions in the crate. If the crate author has provided further descriptions of the functions, you will also see those descriptions in the documentation. This feature makes it really easy to refer to the documentation for all of the crates that you use in your project.

```
$ cargo doc          # generate docs
$ cargo doc --open  # open local docs in your browser
```

Figure 2-2 shows a sample of what the documentation looks like for the `regex` crate.

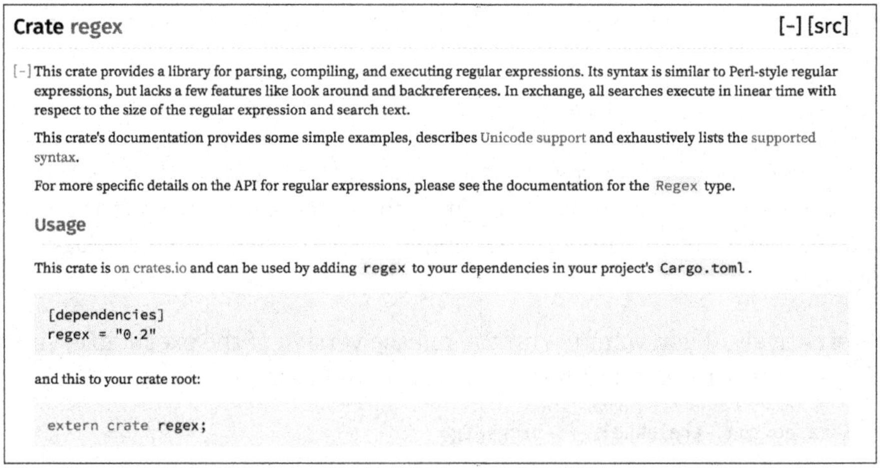
Crate regex [-] [src]

[-] This crate provides a library for parsing, compiling, and executing regular expressions. Its syntax is similar to Perl-style regular expressions, but lacks a few features like look around and backreferences. In exchange, all searches execute in linear time with respect to the size of the regular expression and search text.

This crate's documentation provides some simple examples, describes Unicode support and exhaustively lists the supported syntax.

For more specific details on the API for regular expressions, please see the documentation for the `Regex` type.

Usage

This crate is on crates.io and can be used by adding `regex` to your dependencies in your project's `Cargo.toml`.

```
[dependencies]
regex = "0.2"
```

and this to your crate root:

```
extern crate regex;
```

**Figure 2-2:** Example documentation page from the regex crate

Now that you have an idea of how to create a skeleton crate and how to generate and view the documentation for your dependencies, it would be helpful to find out how to actually add dependencies to your project. You can add dependencies by modifying your *Cargo.toml* manifest file.

# MANIFEST FILE

Cargo uses a file in the top-level directory called *Cargo.toml* to identify and configure projects. Cargo will create one of these with some default sensible contents when you use `cargo new`. The initial configuration is pretty bare though:

```
[package]
name = "myproject"
version = "0.1.0"
authors = ["Your Name <your@email.org>"]
```

We'll go over some of the more common options; you can find full documentation on `doc.crates.io`.

## [package] Section

The package section contains information about the project as a whole. Mainly, the information in the package section is meant to help developers find or use your crates. The three fields provided in the template *Cargo.toml* file are mandatory, but there are many more optional fields:

- description – a short description of your project. The project description will be one of the first statements that a developer sees, after the crate name, to give the developer some idea what the crate is meant to do. A good description will help lead people to use your crate.
- keywords – a set of keywords that can also be used to find your crate on `crates.io`. So, for a crate such as the `serde` crate for serialization, "serialization" is one of the keywords provided. The keywords are another set of search terms that will match your crate.
- documentation – a URL that points to the documentation for your crate. If your `myproject` crate has been pushed to `crates.io`, then you can put `https://docs.rs/myproject` and it will redirect to the documentation for the latest version of your crate. This field will provide a link to the documentation on `crates.io`.
- repository – a URL that points to the repository for your crate, such as its GitHub page. This field will provide a link to the repository on `crates.io`.

- homepage – a URL that points to the homepage for your crate. This field will provide a link to the homepage on `crates.io`.
- license or license-file – These fields provide licensing information for the crate. You can find valid licenses at `http://spdx.org/licenses/`, or you can provide a custom license file as part of the crate directory tree.

```
[package]
# ....

# A short description of the project
description = "..."

# Links to more information about the project
documentation = "..."
homepage = "..."
repository = "..."

# Path to the readme file for the project
readme = "..."

# Short list of keywords for the project
keywords = ["...", "..."]

# Name of the license for the project. List of valid # licenses can be
found at http://spdx.org/licenses/
license = "..."

# Path to a license file if you are using a
# non-standard license.
license-file = "…"
```

After filling in the descriptive information about your crate, you may want to add some additional dependent crates so that you can use all of the functionalities that other developers have written and published to `crates.io`. Those dependencies belong in the dependencies section.

## [dependencies] Section

The main advantage of using Cargo is its easy dependency management. In most cases, dependencies can be defined by adding a single line to your *Cargo.toml* file.

```
[dependencies]
color = "0.6"
```

This is a simple form of a dependency definition used with Cargo. It specifies that the project depends on the color package as pulled from `crates.io`.

The "0.6" in the example specifies that that project depends on any 0.6.x version published. Cargo will automatically use the most recent version, as long as the version starts with "0.6".

If want to use a dependency that is not on `crates.io`, then you can use the full version for dependency definitions like this:

```
[dependencies]
color = { git = "https://github.com/bjz/color-rs" }
geometry = { path = "crates/geometry" }
```

By specifying our dependencies using the full form, Cargo allows us to be a bit more flexible as to where the dependent crates come from. The `color` crate is using a Git dependency and pulls the crate from the latest master commit of the specified Git repository. The `geometry` crate is specified as a path dependency. A path dependency specifies a crate in a path relative to the *Cargo.toml* file.

In the simple form of dependency definitions, we simply specify the version number of the crate that we want to fetch and stated that Cargo automatically uses the "most recent version that starts with 0.6." But what does it mean to say the most recent version? Well, semantic versioning defines precisely what "most recent" means.

## SEMANTIC VERSIONING

Cargo uses and enforces a versioning system called "Semantic Versioning" on the crates that it manages. Semantic versioning, or SemVer, adds specific semantics to the version numbers. For a precise definition of SemVer, see `http://semver.org` for the community, agreed-upon definition of SemVer. For our purposes, however, a basic definition will suffice. Suppose you are presented with a version number that looks like this:

```
2.1.0
```

This version has a "major" component of "2", a "minor" component of "1" and a "patch" component of "0". How each component is changed reflects the type of changes between versions.

A change in the major version portion indicates a complete API incompatibility. However, you should not expect code to work with older or newer major versions of a crate. An example of an API incompatibility would be a public type or public function signature change.

A change in the minor version section indicates a backwards-compatible addition to the crate. Code using the new features will not work with older minor versions, but should work with newer minor versions. So, if you added a new public function to the crate to introduce new functionality without changing any of the existing public function signatures or types, then you could bump the minor version number.

A change in the patch version section indicates a backwards-compatible improvement or bug fix. Code should work with all patch versions of a crate. Patch level changes should not in any way change the public interface to a crate. Implementation changes are acceptable as long as they do not exhibit any user-visible changes beyond the correction of a faulty implementation.

Note that crates with a major version number of 0 are defined as still in initial development. This means that the public API should not be considered stable and that anything could change at any time between versions. Typically, developers will keep compatibility for patch level changes and reserve breaking changes for the minor bumps, but there are no guarantees with a major version of 0.

## PUBLISHING CRATES

You have started work on a new crate, built it, and run it to ensure that it works. Now, you want to share it with the world so that others can benefit from your hard work, just as you have benefited from the work of authors of the crates you used from `crates.io`. You have decided that you want to publish your crate as well. How do you go about doing this?

The simplest possible way to make your crate available for others to use is to push your project to a public Git repository on GitHub or some other public-facing server. Then, anyone with read access to the Git repository can use your crate by specifying a Git dependency that points to the repository that hosts your crate. The main issue with this approach, though, is one of discoverability. How can other developers find your crate for use? Beyond a simple web search and getting lucky, or even word-of-mouth, there is no standard way for Rust developers to discover Git repository-backed crates. There must be a better way.

Luckily, the Rust community has built `crates.io`. We have already encountered `crates.io` since we have specified dependencies in our sample project that are pulled from `crates.io`. Beyond simply serving up dependencies, `crates.io` also provides a way of searching for crates based on name or keywords and provides a view of some of the metadata found in the crate's manifest file. Cargo provides tools that allow you to push your crate up to `crates.io`, just like it provides the means to download crates when you are building a project.

Before you can push your own crate, you must create an account on `crates.io`. The homepage has an obvious link at the top to login with GitHub. Once you do that, you can access your account settings and copy the API access token that you will need to pass on to Cargo so that it can log in to `crates.io` as you.

```
$ cargo login 280c38b98aaeba7d549a261a80d56eRh
```

Once you have logged in once, Cargo will cache the access token so you do not have to log in every time. The next step is to actually publish your crate! Note, however, that crate names are reserved on a first-come, first-served basis. If you try to publish a crate whose name already exists on `crates.io`, and you are not the owner of that name, then the publish will fail.

```
$ cargo publish
```

Now that your crate is published, you should be able to find it by searching for it by name on `crates.io`. If you found it, congratulations! Other people will be able to find it and use it as well.

## EXPANSION COMMANDS FOR CARGO

Cargo has many built-in commands – more than we have space to explain here. The Cargo documentation at `http://doc.crates.io/` is excellent and will further explain the Cargo commands, additional fields that can be set in the manifest file, and more. Be sure to explore it fully. That being said, there are a few expansion commands for Cargo that can be useful to install.

### Cargo Edit

While it is easy to manually edit the Cargo manifest file to add and remove dependencies, it does require a few steps. First, you need to look up the crate on `crates.io` to find the latest version of the crate. Then, you have to get the syntax just right to specify the dependency in the manifest file. The cargo-edit crate is a shortcut to simplify this process. It provides commands to add and remove crates to your manifest file:

```
$ cargo install cargo-edit # installs cargo-edit commands

$ cargo add regex # gets latest version of regex crate

$ cargo add serde@1.0 # gets version 1.0.x of serde crate

$ cargo rm regex # removes the regex crate from manifest

$ cargo list # lists the crates in your manifest

$ cargo list --tree # lists full dependency tree
```

None of the commands provided are absolutely required; you can do all of these modifications yourself and get the same information it provides out of the *Cargo.lock* file. These commands are simply shortcuts that will save you a bit of time.

### Cargo Fmt

When collaborating on software projects with other people, it is typically useful to have a common code style that everyone agrees on. This minimizes the amount of time that developers spend making visual changes to the codebase that do not provide any functional benefits. The `rustfmt` tool is a code style checker and reformatter for Rust code. Additionally, the rustfmt tool provides a Cargo command that can be used to run rustfmt across the source files of your crate.

```
$ cargo install rustfmt # installs the rustfmt commands

$ cargo fmt -- --write-mode=diff # write a diff of the

                                 # changes to standard

                                 # out, also setting an

                                 # error code

$ cargo fmt # simply reformat the code to your code style
```

The `rustfmt` command, callable through `cargo fmt`, provides several different modes:

- replace – format the text into the existing file after creating a backup
- overwrite – format the text into the existing file *without* first creating a backup
- display – simply display the formatted contents of the file to the screen
- diff – produce a display of the differences between the current file and the properly displayed one *and* provide an error code if any changes had to be made
- plain – write to the screen without any metadata
- checkstyle – produce a display of the differences in checkstyle format, used by some continuous integration tools

The two that are the most useful are the `diff` mode and the `overwrite` mode (the default). As seen in Figure 2-3, the `diff` mode will show the differences between your code and the properly formatted code to standardize, as well as set an error code if it would have made any changes. This mode is imminently useful in a continuous integration environment to ensure that all committed code matches the defined code style. The `diff` mode is more flexible than the `checkstyle` mode because `diff` mode does not require any fancy XML parsing to handle the file like checkstyle does. The default `overwrite` mode simply reformats your source code to the code style, in place. Running that before you commit will keep your code in the common style. There are several configuration options for code style that can be defined for use with `rustfmt`, so be sure to check out the documentation.

**Figure 2-3:** Example rustfmt output

```
Diff in /Users/jonathan/Documents/Programming Rust/src/chapter_03/demo_struct/src/main.rs at line 1:
 struct Foo {⏎
     a: i32,⏎
-    b: String⏎
+    b: String,⏎
 }⏎
 ⏎
 fn main() {⏎
Diff in /Users/jonathan/Documents/Programming Rust/src/chapter_03/demo_struct/src/main.rs at line 7:
     let foo = Foo {⏎
         a: 0,⏎
-        b: String::new()⏎
+        b: String::new(),⏎
     };⏎
 ⏎
     println!("a: {}, b: {}", foo.a, foo.b);⏎
```

## Cargo Release

Cargo makes it easy to publish crates to `crates.io`, but there is more to a release than just publishing the crate. Version numbers need to be bumped, tags need to be made, and all of these need to be pushed to your upstream Git repository so that collaborators are kept up to date. That is where the cargo-release crate comes in. Its purpose is to standardize the release process so that you follow a consistent set of steps to release a new version of a crate.

```
$ cargo install cargo-release

$ cargo release --level minor -sign
```

The example cargo release command will:

- bump the minor version number in the manifest,
- generate a GPG-signed commit of the version bump,
- publish the crate to `crates.io`,
- create a GPG-signed tag of the version pushed to `crates.io`
- bump the version number to the next development pre-release version,
- generate a GPG-signed commit of the pre-release bump, and
- push the Git repository (including the tags) to the default upstream remote.

As you can see, there are a lot of details that the cargo release command handles for you. There are more options that you can pass to the command as a custom section called `package.metadata.release` in your *Cargo.toml*. Here are a few of the common ones:

| | |
|---|---|
| sign-commit | A boolean to specify whether or not to sign your commits. |
| tag-message | A template string to use in the tag commit message. You can specify `{{version}}` and `{{prefix}}` in the message and they will be filled in. |
| (pre/pro)-release-commit-message | A template string to use in the pre- or post- commit message. You can specify `{{version}}` in the message and it will be filled in. |
| no-dev-version | A boolean to specify whether or not to bump to a development version after release. |

## KEY TAKEAWAYS

- Crates are the Rust community's flavor of packages.
- Cargo is the Rust community's tool to build, test, and share crates with others.
- Cargo tracks, downloads and builds the dependency graph for your crate.
- Cargo requires crates to use semantic versioning so that it can accurately track the dependencies.
- Developers have created useful extensions to Cargo that you can install to give it extra commands to add and remove dependencies, enforce your code style, and keep your release process standardized.

3

# Type System

Rust's type system provides a powerful problem-solving toolset and learning how to use it comprises a large part of this book. Rust's type system is powerful in that it has features such as algebraic data types that are not commonly found in systems programming languages. These powerful features allow programmers to add richer semantic information to their programs in the form of domain-specific types to make it easier to reason with the code that is being written and hence make it easier to solve problems in the language. Finally, the type system provides all of the components you need in the form of primitive types and ways to piece them together into your own composite types. In order to use this toolset properly, however, you must know about the tools it contains. This chapter will introduce these tools and a little about how they work.

## TYPES & VALUES

Modern programming languages commonly associate two pieces of information with a variable – a value and a type. To understand this, take a look at the following code:

```
let x: i32 = 97;
let y: i32 = 3;
let z = x + y;
```

Since Rust is compiled to native code, it will produce a sequence of CPU instructions like this:

```
%0 = load_i32 x;
%1 = load_i32 y;
%2 = add_i32 %0, %1;
store %2, z;
```

Notice that the types have become part of the instructions themselves. The CPU doesn't actually know what types x, y or z are. Instead, it is up to the compiler to generate the appropriate instructions.

Since data carries no intrinsic type information at runtime, we use types to indicate how that data should be interpreted. Types allow us to turn data into values. Given how closely linked types and values are, we often use the two interchangeably, i.e. "pass an i32 to the function" actually means "pass a value of type i32 to the function". Similarly, we often describe properties of types when the properties actually belong to all values of those types.

Rust has what is known as a strong, static type system. In general, type systems can be described along two axes: the strong/weak axis and the static/dynamic axis. These two axes, along with representative programming languages, can be found in Figure 3-1.

**Figure 3-1:** Type system characteristic axes

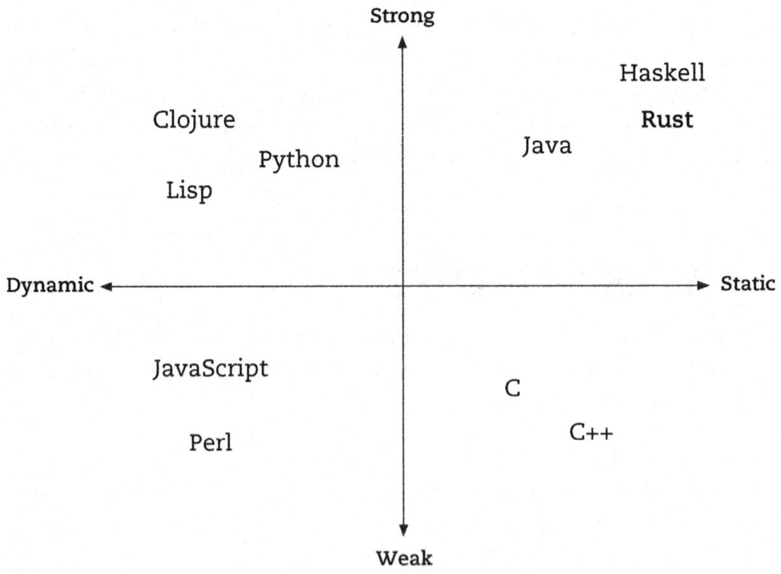

In a weakly typed language, the type of the value is fluid and can change based on how the value is used. In weakly typed languages, you may also have the value "1" being interpreted as a string if you concatenate another string to it, but interpreted as the number 1 if you add another number to it. In a strongly typed language, the type of a value is fixed and cannot change. So, if you have a string value of "1", you can only concatenate strings to it – you cannot add numbers to it and expect the value to act as a number.

Where the strong/weak axis describes the type associated with a value, the static/dynamic axis describes the type of a variable. In a dynamically typed language, a variable does not intrinsically have a type associated with it. Instead, a variable in a dynamically typed language can change its type depending on the value assigned to it. So, a variable that is initialized with a string has the string type, but if you assign a number to that variable, then it will take on the number type. By contrast, with a statically typed language, the type of the variable is fixed when the variable is declared. So, when we say that Rust has a strong, static type system, we mean that values and variables in Rust are very distinct types that are not fluid at run time.

In the next few sections, we will explore Rust's type system and see how Rust allows us to build abstractions from its primitive types and how these primitive types can be combined into composite, algebraic data types.

## PRIMITIVE TYPES

Primitive types are the types that are provided by the language itself, rather than a library. They are the building blocks for more complex, user-defined types. The following table lists the primitive types.

| Type | Notes |
| --- | --- |
| `bool` | Boolean type. Can have a value or either `true` or `false`. |
| `char` | Character type. Represents a single Unicode character and is always four bytes wide to be large enough to encode any Unicode character. |

| Type | Notes |
|---|---|
| `i8, u8`<br>`i16, u16`<br>`i32, u32`<br>`i64, u64` | Fixed width integer types that are either signed (can be negative), or unsigned.<br>Named using the pattern `<signedness><bit width>`, where "`i`" means "signed" and "`u`" means "unsigned". So the integer type `i32` is a 32-bit signed integer |
| `isize, usize` | A "machine-width" integer type. Same as the integer types above, but without a specified size. In general, the size of these integer types is 32-bits on a 32-bit architecture or 64-bits on a 64-bit architecture |
| `f32`<br>`f64` | Floating-point number types. Rust provides IEEE-754 floating-point types in single precision (`f32`) and double precision (`f64`). |
| `&'a T`<br>`&'a mut T` | Immutable and mutable references. The `'a` and `T` are just placeholders for a lifetime and a type, respectively, to be substituted in. |
| `*const T`<br>`*mut T` | Raw pointer types. Provides unchecked access to memory via Rust's `unsafe` mechanism. |
| `[T;N]` | A fixed size array of type `T` with `N` values. |
| `[T]` | The dynamically-sized slice type. |
| `str` | The dynamically-sized string type. |

Many of the types that Rust provides will be familiar to systems programmers. Rust provides basic booleans, fixed-width integers, and floating-point numbers that all correspond to native machine values. Both the raw pointer types and the reference types provide indirect access to memory, much like a native machine index register. All of the types mentioned thus far are common to systems programming languages in one form or another.

Where Rust distinguishes itself is in its fixed-sized array, dynamically-sized slices, and dynamically-sized string types. Compare those types to their cohorts in a language like C. The C programming language claims to have arrays and strings. However, in C, both arrays and strings are really the same type as a pointer; the compiler makes very little distinction between them and generally allows the programmer to use them interchangeably. However, semantically, they are three very different entities and C programmers can encounter problems if they are not careful with their use. Rust gives arrays and strings distinct types from each other *and* from pointers. Additionally, Rust distinguishes between fixed-sized arrays and dynamic arrays to allow the compiler to make additional optimizations.

While primitive types are useful, the abstractions that you can build out of them with a strong type system allows you to encode more semantic information into your program. So, next, let us learn how to define your own types out of the primitive types.

## STRUCTS AND ENUMS

Rust has two basic ways of defining new types – `struct` and `enum`. `struct` is short for "structure" and defines a type that is a composite of some number of component types which can be accessed as fields of the `struct`. Figure 3-2 illustrates a simple struct `Foo` that is the composite of an `i32` and a `String`:

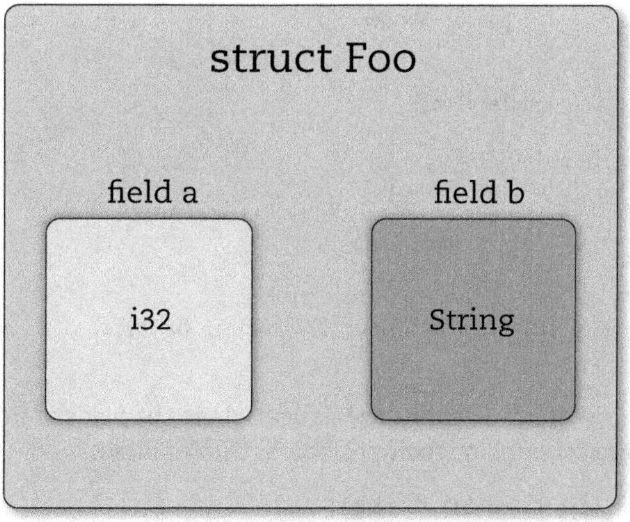


**Figure 3-2:** A simple struct containing two fields

```
struct Foo {
    a: i32,
    b: String
}

fn main() {
    let foo = Foo {
      a: 0,
      b: String::new()
    };

    println!("a: {}, b: {}", foo.a, foo.b);
}
```

The above snippet of code shows a code description of how the struct `Foo` is declared with two fields – `a` and `b` – that have types `i32` and `String`, respectively. You can access those fields using their names as shown. Note, however, that the fields `a` and `b` are only accessible from the function `main` because the `struct Foo` is declared in the same module. If you want to declare a struct that has fields accessible from other modules, you must declare the fields to be public as follows:

```
mod module {
    pub struct Foo {
        pub a: i32,
        pub b: String
    }
}
use module::Foo;

fn main() {
    let foo = Foo {
      a: 0,
      b: String::new()
    };

    println!("a: {}, b: {}", foo.a, foo.b);
}
```

You can also define *tuple* structs where the fields aren't named and instead are accessed by their position in the definition.

```
struct Foo(i32, String);

fn main() {
    let foo = Foo(0, String::new());
```

```
    println!("0: {}, 1: {}", foo.0, foo.1);
}
```

As you can see here, instead of a and b, we use 0 and 1 to access the fields.

Finally, you can define a *unit-like* struct, which has no fields at all:

```
struct Empty;
```

Unit-like structs carry no data and are mainly used when you need a type, but no data. One example of using a unit-like struct is when you want to implement a trait, but your implementation doesn't need to store any information.

enum, short for enumeration, defines a type that contains a number of different options, each of which may be a composite type, just like a struct. Each option is called a *variant*.

```
enum Bar {
    A { name: String },
    B(i32, i32),
    C
}

fn main() {
    let bar = Bar::B(3, 14);
    match bar {
      Bar::A{ name: val } => println!("A({})", val),
      Bar::B(v1, v2) => {
        println!("B({}, {})", v1, v2);
      }
      Bar::C => println!("C"),
    }
}
```

Bar is an enum with three variants, named A, B, and C. The A variant has a single field, called name, with the type String. The B variant has two unnamed fields, both of which are the i32 type. The C variant has no fields at all. Figure 3-3 shows how the enum can be only one variant at a time.

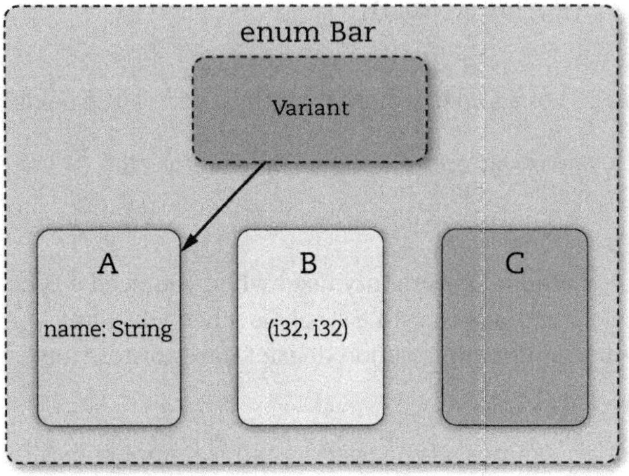


**Figure 3-3:** Simple enum with three variants

Getting at the data inside an enum requires the use of `match`. This is because the variable could be any of the variants and thus, we need to know which one before we access the data. In general, the `enum` type in Rust acts like a tagged union since all of the variants share the same storage in the variable, but only one variant is valid at any given time. The size of an `enum` value is the largest size of any of the variants of the `enum`.

If you look closely at the C variant of the Bar enum above, you can see that it does not have any data associated with it. In fact, if you made an enum where none of the variants had any data associated with it, and squinted really hard at it, it would look much like an enum in the C programming language, so much so that Rust calls it a C-like enum.

## C-Like Enum

There is a special kind of enum called a "C-like enum" (named so because of how it emulates the behavior of `enums` in C). C-like enums are `enum` types where no variant has any fields:

```
enum Cowboy {
    Good,
    Bad,
    Ugly
}
```

What distinguishes them is that you can cast C-like enums to integer types. This is allowed when the domain of the `enum` is smaller than the domain of the integer type you are casting to:

```
fn cowboy_to_int(cowboy: Cowboy) -> i32 {
    cowboy as i32
}
```

However, you cannot do the opposite because the domain of the integer type is much larger than the domain of the enum. That is, there are many values of an integer type that do not correspond to values in the `enum`:

```
fn int_to_cowboy(val: i32) -> Cowboy {
    // error: non-scalar cast 'i32' as 'Cowboy'
    val as Cowboy
}
```

The other thing that sets them apart is that you can define what values the variants have. Normally, the values are assigned incrementally and in order, so that the first variant gets the value '0', the next variant gets the value '1', and so on.

```
enum Rating {
    Awful = -2,
    Bad   = -1,
    Ok    =  0,
    Good  =  1,
    Great =  2
}
```

The values can be any integer; however, each variant must have a unique value.

Why are C-like enums useful? Does it really matter that each variant gets a unique value? If you are writing strictly pure Rust code, then no, C-like enums do not get a lot of use. However, most code has to interact with the outside world. There are two main uses of the C-like enum. First, it makes interfacing with C libraries easier because a C enum is basically just an integer. By defining our C-like enum where the variants are numbered the same as the actual C enum, it makes foreign function code using the enum easier to write. Secondly, it makes serialization of enums out to a file easier. We cannot store a `Rating::Awful` into a file, but we can store the `-2` representation of the `Rating::Awful` into a file. In both cases, the C-like enum is not strictly necessary because we can emulate the same behavior by using a match statement. However, the C-like enum makes our code shorter and more readable.

Looking closely at Figure 3-3 you may have noticed that the definitions of the variants look very similar to how structs are defined. In fact, you can think of an enum type as a collection of structs, where a value of that type is exactly one of those structs. Looking back at our representation of an enum, you can see how the enum looks like three structs combined, with the variant only selecting one of them at a time. In the diagram, the A variant is like a struct that has a single name field, while the B variant is like a tuple struct. Finally, the C variant has no data associated with it, so it is like a unit-like struct.

This leads to the question: could we combine structs and enums? The answer is, yes, under the umbrella of Algebraic Data Types.

## ALGEBRAIC DATA TYPES

Both structs and enums are "Algebraic Data Types", or "ADTs" for short. ADTs have been extensively researched and implemented in functional languages like Haskell and OCaml, but have not seen much use in systems programming languages like C or C++. ADTs bring a bit of mathematical rigor to a programming language's type system. That rigor can be used by developers to prove properties about software written in the language or to automatically generate test cases for property-based testing (see Chapter 9 for more information on property-based testing). Rust is relatively unique in that it brings support for ADTs to a systems programming language.

ADTs unify two ideas that are in many languages considered separate – a value being composed of multiple sub-values (the `struct` concept) and the type of that value being one of a set of types (the `enum` concept). This is a considerably dense statement, so let us unpack it a little.

First, a value being composed of multiple sub-values means that you can look at your value and break it down into smaller parts. For example, the value `(1, 2, false)` is comprised of three sub-values: 1, 2 and false. Each of these sub-values has its own type as well.

Next, the type of a value being one of a set of types means that, even if you do not necessarily know what type your value has, you *do* know that it has to be one of the types in some list. In some languages, this is called a "union" and is written like this:

```
union value_t {
  int i;
  float f;
  char* s;
};
```

Other languages use sub-typing to restrict the list of potential types, though the list isn't known until runtime:

```
interface IValue { ... }

class IntValue implements IValue {
    int i;
}
```

ADTs work by combining the list of possible types with the definition of the sub-values for each type:

```
enum MyValue {
    Int(i32),
    Float(f32),
    String(String)
}
```

A value of type `MyValue` can be one of three types: `i32`, `f32` or `String`. The names associated with each type are there so we can indicate which type we actually want our value to be. Each variant is a value and indicates the types of the values it contains.

## TRAITS

Traits in Rust allow programmers to define interfaces for types to implement so they can be used in generic code. To quickly recap traits, a good example is the standard library trait `Clone`.

```
pub trait Clone: Sized {
    fn clone(&self) -> Self;
    fn clone_from(&mut self, source: &Self) {
        *self = source.clone();
    }
}
```

This trait defines a single required method, `clone`, that takes an immutable reference to `self` and returns a value of the `Self` type. It defines a provided method `clone_from` that takes a mutable reference to `self` and an immutable reference to `Self`. It also requires that all implementers of the `Clone` trait also implement the `Sized` trait.

## Method Receiver

The `&self` in the clone method is called the method "receiver". It indicates that it is a method and how the value is received by the method. `&self` means that the method takes an immutable reference to `self`, `&mut self` means that the method takes a mutable reference to `self` and `self` means that the method takes `self` by-value.

## Self Type

Inside trait definitions, a special type called `Self` is available. `Self` refers to the type implementing that trait. So, for example, if you implement the `Clone` trait on `MyType`, `Self` refers to `MyType`:

```
struct MyType(i32);
impl Clone for MyType {
    fn clone(&self) -> MyType {
        MyType(self.0)
    }
}
```

## Self Bounds

In general, a Bound is a constraint that requires that a type implements the trait specified by the Bound. In the context of a trait definition, a `Self` Bound requires that types implementing the trait also implement the other traits in the Bound. This is sometimes referred to as "Supertraits" because they are similar to the object-oriented concept of superclasses. For example, the `Clone` trait requires that all implementers also implement the `Sized` trait.

## Default Methods

Trait definitions can provide default implementations for certain methods. These are useful when there is an obvious implementation in terms of the other methods on the trait or in terms of methods that are provided by `Self` Bounds on the trait. For example, the `clone_from` method on `Clone` can be implemented in terms of the required `clone` method. However, just because the trait provides a default implementation, it does not mean that your implementation of the trait must use that default implementation. You are free to implement these default methods yourself. For instance, there might be a more efficient way to implement `clone_from` for some types than to fall back to the default implementation and simply call clone on the object.

## Trait Implementation Rules

For any given type, there must be, at most, one implementation of a given trait. This ensures that there is no ambiguity when figuring out which method to use. The main rule about implementing traits is therefore that you cannot implement the same trait on a type multiple times.

There is another rule related to implemented traits that arises from the previous rule. To understand this, let us examine the situation the rule is designed to prevent.

```
// main.rs
extern crate common_1;
extern crate common_2;
use common_1::CommonTrait;
use common_2::CommonType;

impl CommonTrait for CommonType { ... }
```

This code uses two other crates, `common_1` and `common_2` and implements a trait from `common_1` on a type from `common_2`. Assuming that this implementation is not present in either crate, everything works fine. However, if we have another crate – `other` – that also implements `CommonTrait` for `CommonType`, perhaps differently:

```
// other.rs
extern crate common_1;
extern crate common_2;
```

```
use common_1::CommonTrait;
use common_2::CommonType;

impl CommonTrait for CommonType { ... }
```

By itself, this is also fine. What happens if we alter `main.rs` to add `extern crate other`? Well, now there are two implementations of `common_1::CommonTrait` for `common_2::CommonType` available. This violates the main rule of not having more than a single implementation of a trait for a type. To prevent this from happening, Rust has the following rule:

> When implementing a trait for a type, either the trait or the type must be local to the crate containing the implementation.

A "local" type or trait simply means that the crate defines either the type or trait, or both. This would prevent the earlier situation as neither the type nor trait are defined in either `main.rs` or `other.rs`.

What does this mean in practice? Well, the Rust standard library provided several standard traits that can be implemented by types that you define in your crate. For instance, if you were creating a crate that fetched files over HTTP, you could have a type that corresponds to the connection and implement the standard Read trait on that type. Consumers of your crate could then use your HTTP connection type anywhere that a type implementing Read was required.

Likewise, you can create your own trait in your crate and define it for any of the standard types that are provided by Rust. For example, if you were creating a crate that computes digests of a message, you could provide a trait Digest that users of your crate can implement. Additionally, you can implement the Digest trait for all of the basic types that Rust provides to make it easier for consumers of your crate to use the Digest trait.

## GENERIC TYPES

Good programming practice says that common functionality and logic should be factored out into a single location. Strong typing, as found in Rust, means that otherwise-identical code cannot be factored out due to it working with different types. In the following example, we have two data structures that both represent a stack. However, one is a stack of integers and the other is a stack of floating point numbers.

```
struct MyIntStack { ... }

fn push_int(stk: &mut MyIntStack, val: i32) { ... }

struct MyFloatStack { ... }

fn push_float(stk: &mut MyFloatStack,
              val: f32) { ... }
```

These types and functions look very similar to a signature standpoint, except that one uses i32 types and the other uses f32 types. They cannot be combined because the types are different. Generic types allow us to abstract the type itself, the same way a function allows us to abstract an input value to some code.

```
struct MyStack<T> { ... }
fn push<T>(stk: &mut MyStack<T>, val: T) { ... }
```

Here, we see a type with a type parameter and a function with a type parameter. Type parameters are key, so this is where we will start.

## Type Parameters

Refactoring is a common task while building software. Patterns repeated in code can often be isolated and moved to a single location. In doing so, you need to ensure that the data the code needs is available. This is normally done using function arguments, so values can be passed in by the calling code.

Type parameters are similar in that they ensure the type you are factoring out is still available in some form. You can have type parameters almost anywhere you can have types: `struct` and `enum` definitions, trait definitions, function declarations and even type aliases.

```
struct Foo<T>(T);
enum Bar<T> {
  A(T),
  B
}
trait Baz<T> { ... }
```

```
fn foo<T>(x: &T) { ... }
type Foobar<T> = (Foo<T>, Bar<T>);
```

Type parameters define "holes" for types to be substituted into. Each unique set of substitutions defines a new type. For example, `Foo<i32>` is a different type to `Foo<&str>`. The implication of this is that using something with unsubstituted type parameters is an error.

## Trait Bounds

There are two ideas of Rust that are important when talking about generic types:

1. Type-checking a function call which requires looking only at the function's type-signature, and
2. A generic function is valid for all types that can be substituted in the type parameters.

One consequence of this is that an unconstrained type parameter greatly restricts how much the generic code can do with it. Often, we need to restrict which types can be used with the function to ensure that the values provide certain functionality. This is where trait bounds come in.

As we saw earlier, traits define an interface that types can choose to provide by implementing the trait. Trait bounds allow code to require that any type substituted for a given type parameter implements the traits listed.

```
fn duplicate<T: Clone>(val: T) -> (T, T) {
    let val1 = val.clone();
    let val2 = val;
    (val1, val2)
}
```

This function duplicates the value given to it by calling the `clone` method. This works for any type that implements the `Clone` trait as indicated by the bound `T: Clone` in the function's signature. The bound lets Rust know that, no matter what type `T` ends up being, a call to the `clone` method is always valid. It is worth noting, though, that putting a trait bound on a type does not restrict the type to *only* having the bound trait implemented on it. Rather, it is a minimum set of requirements on the type before it can be used generically in the function.

## Generic Traits and Blanket Implementations

Traits without type parameters are simple to implement:

```
struct MyStruct;
impl Clone for MyStruct {
    fn clone(&self) -> MyStruct {
        MyStruct
    }
}
```

Since a trait with substituted type parameters is a unique trait, it is similarly simple:

```
struct SpecialNum(i32);
impl From<i32> for SpecialNum {
    fn from(val: i32) -> SpecialNum {
        SpecialNum(val)
    }
}
```

Since `From<i32>` is distinct from `From<i8>`, the following implementation does not conflict:

```
impl From<i8> for SpecialNum {
    fn from(val: i8) -> SpecialNum {
        SpecialNum(val as i32)
    }
}
```

However, it is possible to use type parameters in implementations:

```
trait Foo<T> { ... }
struct Bar { ... }

impl<T> Foo<T> for Bar { ... }
```

You should read that last line as "for all types, `T`, implement `Foo<T>` for `Bar`". This kind of implementation is most useful when combined with trait bounds:

```
impl<T: Qux> Foo<T> for Bar { ... }
```

As explained earlier, bounds allow the code to do more with a type parameter, so it's uncommon for a generic trait implementation to use unbounded type parameters.

Type parameters can also be used in the type part of the implementation:

```
struct Foo<T>(T);
impl<T: Clone> Clone for Foo<T> {
    fn clone(&self) -> Foo<T> {
        Foo(self.0.clone())
    }
}
```

Here we can read the implementation line as "for all types, T, that implement `Clone`, implement the `Clone` trait on `Foo<T>`". You can also implement traits on type parameters themselves:

```
trait MyTrait : Clone { ... }

impl<T: Clone> MyTrait for T { ... }
```

These are called "blanket implementations".

## Associated Types

Operator overloading in Rust is implemented using traits. For each overloadable operator, there is a corresponding trait that can be implemented for that operator. The most obvious definition of the trait for multiplication is this:

```
trait Mul<RHS, Res> {
    fn mul(self, other: RHS) -> Res;
}
```

In this example definition of the `Mul` trait, the left-hand side of the multiplication would be the `Self` type and the right-hand side of the multiplication would be a generic type we are calling `RHS`. The result of the multiplication is a generic type we are calling `Res`. This example trait allows multiplication to be implemented with different types for both the input and the output, providing the most flexibility. However, it poses an issue when the Rust compiler tries to perform type inference. Consider the following code:

```
let a: T = ...;
let b: U = ...;
let x = a * b;
```

When the compiler sees this code, it looks for an implementation of the `Mul` trait for the types involved. We have `a: T` and `b: U` so we look for an implementation of `Mul<U, ?>` on type `T`. That `?` is the return type of the multiplication and, therefore, the type of `x`. But we did not specify the type for `x`, so it has to be inferred and this poses a problem because we allowed the result type to be generic. We need to know the type of `x` in order to find the correct version of the `Mul` trait, but we need the `Mul` trait to determine the type of `x`. We could explicitly specify the type for `x`, but that only solves the problem in this specific instance.

Instead, one observation you can make is that the output type of multiplication is determined by the two input types. If we did not require the result type of the multiplication when finding a `Mul` implementation, everything would work as expected.

This is where associated types come in. Associated types are types that are associated with a specific implementation of a trait. The version of Mul written using associated types looks like this:

```
trait Mul<RHS> {
    type Output;
    fn mul(self, other: RHS) -> Self::Output;
}
```

This solves our problem because the result type is no longer part of the trait's type parameters. Let us use this new definition of `Mul` to take another look at our example.

```
let a: T = ...;
let b: U = ...;
let x = a * b;

impl Mul<U> for T {
    type Output = V;
    fn mul(self, other: U) -> V { ... }
}
```

Now, when Rust looks for an implementation of `Mul`, its instead trying to find an implementation of `Mul<U>` for `T`. We find the implementation and select it as the one to use. Now that we have an implementation, we can use it to determine the type of `x`, which is `V`.

## Where Clauses

Where clauses are a way of specifying more advanced constraints on types. They can be used in place of regular trait bounds, but can also be used to bound more complex types and even reverse bounds where the type parameter is restricted based on implementations for a concrete type.

The simplest use of where clauses is to write out regular bounds in a different way:

```
fn foo<T: Clone,
       E: Handle<T> + Clone,
       A: Op<(T, E)> + Clone>(a: &mut A) { ... }
```

becomes:

```
fn foo<T, E, A>(a: &mut A)
      where T: Clone,
      E: Handle<T> + Clone,
      A: Op<(T, E)> + Clone
{ ... }
```

For large type parameter lists and complex bounds, where clauses can be much easier to read.

If you want to add a bound to an associated type, where clauses are the only way to do it:

```
fn foo<I>(iter: I)
      where I: Iterator,
      I::Item: Clone
{ ... }
```

This indicates that the `Item` associated type of the `Iterator` implementation for `I` must implement the `Clone` trait.

Where clauses can also be used to bound other types:

```
fn foo<T, U>(t: T, u: U)
      where (T, U): Value
{ ... }
```

Here, we are indirectly constraining the types of `T` and `U` to where there is an implementation of the `Value` trait for the type `(T, U)`. Neither `T` nor `U` are required to implement any specific traits, just the combination of them in `(T, U)`.

Finally, you can use where clauses to constrain type parameters based on the existence of an implementation of a trait on a concrete type:

```
fn foo<S>(s: S) where String: Into<S> { ... }
```

Here, we are indicating that `String` must implement the trait `Into<S>`. This indirectly constrains the type parameter `S` to where that statement is true.

## DYNAMICALLY SIZED TYPES

Most types have a known size. That is, the number of bytes a given type takes up in memory is known at compile time. For example, an `i32` has a size of 4 bytes. This property is important as the compiler often needs to know these sizes when compiling code. When information is known at compile time, it is considered to be known "statically".

In contrast, some types have a size that is not known at compile time. The size of the type has to be determined at runtime. These types are called "dynamically sized types", or DSTs, as the size has to be found dynamically.

Dynamically sized types seem to conflict with the idea that the compiler needs to know the sizes of types statically. Though this is true, the compiler only needs to know the sizes of types in certain circumstances. If we never use DSTs in a way that requires the size to be known, everything can work fine. Here are a few places where the compiler needs to know the size of a type statically:

- Storing it in a variable
- Storing it in a data structure
- Passing it as function argument
- Returning it from a function

This seems rather limiting as those places correspond to almost everything you might want to do with a value. We work around this by employing a technique called "indirection". Indirection is where data is referred to indirectly. Instead of having a variable containing a DST, you have a variable that contains something you can use to access the data. The simplest form of indirection (and the one Rust uses for DSTs) is using pointers.

Pointers are always the same size, no matter what they are pointing to. This means we don't need to go and find the size of the thing pointed to, as it does not matter. However, we still need to know the sizes of the types dynamically so pointers to DSTs carry around some extra information we can use to figure out that size. Since pointers to DSTs have more data than other pointers, they are called "fat pointers".

Any pointer can be used for indirection – from the built-in `&T` and `*mut T`, to the standard library's smart pointers, `Box<T>` and `Rc<T>`.

## Primitive DSTs

There are three "primitive" DSTs: `[T]` `str` and `Trait.` You can build your own dynamically sized types from these, but these three are the building blocks you use.

`[T]` represents a contiguous sequence of `T` elements in memory. As they are a dynamically sized type, the number of elements is not known at compile time.

`str` is similar to `[T]` in that it represents a sequence of elements. `str` specifically represents a sequence of bytes, restricted so they form a UTF-8 encoded string.

`Trait` is the odd one out, as it does not actually name a specific type. Instead, it represents the fact that all traits are themselves types.

You are not restricted to just the primitive DSTs – you can create your own custom DST out of the primitive DSTs.

## User-defined DSTs

Dynamically sized types are not just limited to the primitive ones above. You can define types that are themselves dynamically sized:

```
struct FilePath([u8]);
```

`FilePath` is a DST because it contains a `[u8]`, which is itself a DST. There are two rules for defining your own dynamically sized types:

1. Only structs can have DST fields.
2. There can only be one dynamically-sized field and it must be the last one.

As the second rule implies, you can have extra fields in a DST struct:

```
struct DataBlock {
    id: usize,
    owner: OwnerID,
    data: [u8]
}
```

As long as the DST field is the final field in the struct, everything works fine.

It is more common to have possibly-DST fields when working with generic types. The same rules apply.

```
struct RcInner<T: ?Sized> {
    count: usize,
    val: T
}
```

`RcInner` is the actual data for a reference counted smart pointer. It contains the count and the value stored.

What is that funny ?Sized tacked onto the end of the type parameter for? Since it is a smart pointer, we want to be able to use it for indirection, so we remove the Sized bound with ?Sized. Note, however, that this does not necessarily make RcInner a DST – it merely allows it to potentially be an unsized type (a DST), depending on what type is substituted into T. RcInner<i32> is a sized type, whereas RcInner<[i32]> is a DST.

## The Sized Bound

You may have found that this code does not work:

```
fn foo<T>(x: &T) { ... }

let list: &[i32] = ...;
foo(list);
```

It therefore gives you this error message:

```
error: the trait 'Sized' is not implemented for the type '[i32]'
```

Where does this Sized trait come from? The function does not mention Sized as a bound, so why is it required? It is because Rust inserts an implicit Sized bound on type parameters. In the vast majority of cases, code assumes that a type parameter is sized, so if the Sized bound had to be added explicitly, most code would need to add it. Instead, Rust conveniently adds it on for you. Beyond that, you cannot actually implement the Sized trait yourself. Instead, all types that are statically sized (that are not DSTs) implicitly implement the Sized trait. In the error message above, the compiler is telling you that you defined a generic function that has a type with a bound on Sized, but you are passing a DST to the function (which does not implement Sized).

We can correct this error, though. Sometimes, you do want to accept DSTs, so Rust allows you to remove the Sized bound with some special syntax:

```
fn foo<T: ?Sized>(x: &T) { ... }

let list: &[i32] = ...;
foo(list);
```

This syntax states "`foo` is generic in type `T` which is optionally `Sized`". The `Sized` trait is the only trait allowed to use this special syntax. The relaxation of the `Sized` trait allows the example to type-check.

## KEY TAKEAWAYS

- Rust provides a large selection of primitive types and the means to easily create your own compound types using Algebraic Data Types.
- Traits are Rust-speak for an interface that can be implemented for a specific type.
- Generic functions operate on types. Usually, generic functions require that types implement one or more traits that the function can use.
- Dynamically sized types tend to rear their heads when instantiating a generic function. In those cases, you might have to relax the `Sized` bound on the generic type used by the function so that you can pass a DST in.

4

# Extending Types

Rust's standard library contains a variety of common functionalities used by most programs. However, sometimes the functionality is missing, or the behavior is different than what you want. Rather than having to replicate the hard work that went into the standard library, what if you could simply add the functionality that you need? This chapter will demonstrate how to add functionality to foreign types using traits, alter the behavior of foreign types using wrapper types and extend traits using extension traits.

### What is a "foreign type"?

This chapter will talk a lot about "foreign types" and "foreign traits". For something to be "foreign" in a Rust context, it means that it was defined in a different crate to the one you are writing. So, anything you use from the standard library is "foreign".

## Extending Types with Traits

Sometimes, you find yourself wanting to add functionality to foreign types. Maybe you want to provide a nice API to your users, or maybe you want to extend the functionality the type already has. In any case, Rust provides an easy way to do so – traits.

You can implement a trait on a type if either the trait or the type is local to the current crate. Rust enforces this restriction so that there is only one implementation of a given trait for a given type. In this case, the type is foreign, so we have to use a local trait to write the implementation.

## ADDING FUNCTIONALITY

Sometimes, a foreign type does not quite provide the functionality you want and you find yourself wanting to extend it. Rather than replicate the work already done, we can use a trait to add the functionality to the existing type.

For example, let us say you want to add support for trigonometric functions (sin, cos, tan, etc.) to the integer types. Since the integer types are considered foreign to your crate, you have to use a trait to extend the types.

```
trait TrigOps {
  fn sin(self) -> f64;
  fn cos(self) -> f64;
  fn tan(self) -> f64;
}
```

Here, we are defining methods for just the three main trigonometry functions. Each one takes self by-value to match the same methods on the floating-point types. We return `f64`, rather than `Self`, because all of them return a value between -1 and 1, meaning that an integer return would not be too useful.

The implementation for each integer type will look the same, so we will only consider one of them – `i32`.

```
impl TrigOps for i32 {
  fn sin(self) -> f64 {
    (self as f64).sin()
  }
  fn cos(self) -> f64 {
    (self as f64).cos()
  }
  fn tan(self) -> f64 {
    (self as f64).tan()
  }
}
```

All we are doing is casting the integer, `self`, to `f64` and using the appropriate method on it. This allows us to write `123.sin()` without getting an error.

## EXTENDING COLLECTIONS

One common case is when you want to extend functionality of some local type to collections containing that type.

```
struct Value {
    name: String,
    id: isize
}

impl Value {
  fn print(&self) {
    print!("({}[{}])", self.name, self.id);
  }
}
```

Here, we have a simple type with a single method that prints out some information about the value. We want to extend this behavior so you can call `print` on `&[Value]` and `HashMap<String, Value>`. The first thing to do is to move the functionality to a trait:

```
trait PrintValue {
  fn print(&self);
}

impl PrintValue for Value {
  fn print(&self) {
    print!("({}[{}])", self.name, self.id);
  }
}
```

This simply defines a trait, `PrintValue`, with the method we want and implements on the `Value` type. Next, we want to implement the trait for `[Value]`:

```
impl PrintValue for [Value] {
  fn print(&self) {
    let mut first = true;
    print!("[");
    for val in self {
```

```
      if !first {
        print!("\n ");
      }
      val.print();
      first = false;
    }
    print!("]");
  }
}
```

This implementation will print out something like this:

```
[(Apple[1234])
 (Cherry[5420])
 (Banana[256])]
```

One thing to note for is that the implementation is on [Value]. This allows the print method to not only be called on [Value], but also on anything that dereferences to [Value]. This includes Vec<Value> as well as fat pointer types such as Box<[Value]> and Rc<[Value]>.

The HashMap<String, Value> implementation is next:

```
use std::collections::HashMap;

impl PrintValue for HashMap<String, Value> {
  fn print(&self) {
    let mut first = true;
    print!("{{");
    for (key, val) in self {
      if !first {
        print!("\n ");
      }
      print!("{}: ", key);
      val.print();
      first = false;
    }
    print!("}}");
  }
}
```

This implementation will print something like this:

```
{A: (Aardvark[912])
 B: (Bird[858])
 C: (Cat[101])}
```

We have achieved our initial goal of being able to generically call print on collections by implementing PrintValue for them, but let us take it a little further. If you look, you will see that the only method from Value we actually use is the print method from the PrintValue trait. This means that we do not actually need something of type Value – just anything that implements the PrintValue trait. We can update our PrintValue implementations as follows:

```
impl<V: PrintValue> PrintValue for [V] { ... }
impl<V: PrintValue> PrintValue for
        HashMap<String, V> { ... }
```

All we have done was replace the Value type from the previous implementations with a V type parameter bounded by the PrintValue trait. This allows you to call print on things like Vec<HashMap<String, Value>>.

## CONVERSION TRAITS

The standard library provides a number of traits for basic conversion between types. The main two are Into and From; however, since there is a blanket implementation that provides an Into implementation for every From implementation, we will focus on From.

You might be wondering why we are looking at traits from the standard library when we already established that we need a local trait. To answer that, let us first take a quick look at the From trait:

```
trait From<T>: Sized {
  fn from(T) -> Self;
}
```

The important thing to note here is that `From` is generic. Generic traits deviate from the regular definition-based rule for determining local vs. foreign. For our purposes, we can add this exception for generic traits:

> Generic traits with type parameters substituted using local types are considered local traits.

What this means is that even though `From<T>` is defined in a foreign crate, `From<MyType>` is local, if `MyType` is local.

Let us look at an example:

```
use numbers::Int;

impl From<Int> for i32 {
  fn from(i: Int) -> i32 {
    i.to_isize() as i32
  }
}
```

Here, `Int` is some special integer type that is defined in our `numbers` module, with at least the method `to_isize`. We want to be able to convert to the built-in integers using the standard conversion traits. Since `Int` is a local type, `From<Int>` is a local trait, and therefore the implementation above is allowed. This allows users to write `i32::from(myint)`. Additionally, users can use the default `Into<T>` implementation and get `into` for free after implementing `From<Int>`:

```
let val: i32 = myint.into();
```

Back when we were defining the `TrigOps` trait, we stated that the implementation for each integer will look the same. We can actually remove a lot of duplication by taking advantage of that fact and using the `Into<T>` trait. The `Into<T>` trait is useful for automatically converting between types. Before, we cast the `i32` integer self to a `f64` and then called the appropriate method. What if, instead, we implemented the trait for any type that could be converted into a `f64`? This will allow us to simplify our implementation to look like the following:

```
impl<T: Into<f64>> TrigOps for T {
    fn sin(self) -> f64 {
        self.into().sin()
    }

    fn cos(self) -> f64 {
        self.into().cos()
    }

    fn tan(self) -> f64 {
        self.into().tan()
    }
}
```

This implementation also has the added benefit that any type, even custom types, that implement the `Into<f64>` trait, will be able to use our `TrigOps` trait.

Extending the functionality of existing types is great, but what if you want to alter the functionality instead? You may want to implement a trait on that type differently to how it is already implemented or alter the guarantees that the type provides. This is where "wrapper types" come in.

## Wrapper Types

Wrapper types are completely new, distinct types from the type being wrapped. There are two main advantages of wrapper types. Primarily, wrapper types are stronger versions of type aliases since they are distinct types; they provide the same semantic information that a type alias provides by giving a domain specific name to the type. But, since wrapper types are distinct, the underlying type cannot be directly used like it could be with a type alias. This provides you with stronger type protection in your programs. Additionally, since wrapper types are distinct types, any methods available to the wrapped type are not on the wrapper. This allows you to implement new methods and traits on the wrapper, but any underlying functionality needs to be exposed manually.

Most wrapper types look a little like this:

```
struct Id(u32);
```

While not required, wrapper types are normally tuple-like structs with a single field of the type being wrapped. While we could write the type like this:

```
struct Id {
  id: u32
}
```

using a tuple struct reinforces the fact that this is just a wrapper as it visually looks like a wrapper around the existing type. Additionally, using a tuple struct as the wrapper type makes it visually simpler to construct a new instance of the type to pass into a function.

By creating a wrapper type, we want to distinguish between two types that have the same physical representation, but are different semantically. This typically means that the types need to behave differently. We can make the wrapper types behave differently than their underlying types by re-implementing some of the standard traits to provide different behavior than the base type provides.

## RE-IMPLEMENTING TRAITS

Built-in integers have a fixed number of bits, which means that some mathematical operations will result in values too big to store in that number of bits. There are a few ways to handle this possibility, with the most common way being to "overflow", or just drop, the extra bits that do not fit. This is equivalent to this calculation, where we only have enough space for three decimal digits:

```
900 + 250 = 150
```

What has happened is that the thousands place has been dropped, as the result "overflowed" the space given.

Another way to handle this case is called "saturation". Saturation is when the result goes to the maximum or minimum value and then stays there. The example above would instead look like this:

```
900 + 250 = 999
```

The maximum value we can fit into three decimal digits is 999, since the result of the addition would be greater than that, we “saturate” the result and return 999.

By default, Rust integers use overflow to handle this situation. However, we can use wrapper types to change this behavior to saturating:

```
#[derive(Copy, Clone)]
use std::ops::Add;

struct Saturating(pub u32);
impl Add<Saturating> for Saturating {
  type Output = Saturating;

  fn add(self, rhs: Saturating) -> Saturating {
    let result = self.0.checked_add(rhs.0);
    if let Some(val) = result {
      Saturating(val)
    } else {
      Saturating(u32::max_value())
    }
  }
}
```

Here, we are using the `checked_add` method to see if the result overflowed. `checked_add` returns `Option<u32>`, using `None` to signal overflow. We also implement the `Copy` and `Clone` traits using derive in order to get the same behavior as the underlying `u32`.

## TYPE SAFETY

One advantage of having a strong type system is that it can be used to catch issues during compilation rather than relying on testing. Let us look at an example:

```
use std::sync::atomic::{
    AtomicUsize,
    ATOMIC_USIZE_INIT,
    Ordering
};

static ID_COUNTER: AtomicUsize = ATOMIC_USIZE_INIT;
```

```
fn get_id() -> usize {
    ID_COUNTER.fetch_add(1, Ordering::SeqCst)
}

fn use_id(id: usize) {
    let new_id = get_id();
    assert_ne!(new_id, id);
    /* Do stuff with distinct id and new_id */
}
```

This code generates unique ID numbers using a global variable, manipulated using atomic operations. The `fetch_add` method on an `AtomicUsize` adds the given number to the stored value and returns the previous value. This is done atomically, so that two threads generating IDs at the same time would not get the same values. The `Ordering::SeqCst` simply gives a strong guarantee that the threads see consecutive operations in the same order and is not really important to the discussion at hand.

The `use_id` function takes one of those IDs in order to perform its function. One assumption it makes is that `new_id` and `id` are always different. However, what if we did this?

```
let id = get_id();
use_id(id + 1);
```

While there is no guarantee that the next `get_id` will return `id + 1`, it is possible, invalidating the assumption that `use_id` makes and potentially causes bugs. While we can always say "do not do that", how about making it impossible to do it in the first place? The following code shows one way to do this:

```
use std::sync::atomic::{
    AtomicUsize,
    ATOMIC_USIZE_INIT,
    Ordering};

#[derive(Copy, Clone, PartialEq)]
pub struct Id(usize);

impl Id {
  pub fn get() -> Id {
    static COUNTER: AtomicUsize = ATOMIC_USIZE_INIT;

    Id(COUNTER.fetch_add(1, Ordering::SeqCst))
  }
```

```
    pub fn get_inner(self) -> usize {
      self.0
    }
  }

  fn use_id(id: Id) { ... }
```

Now, we have an Id struct wrapping a usize. Since we have our own type to attach functionality to, the get_id function has become the Id::get associated function.

Id has less functionality than the usize it wraps. You cannot do arithmetic on an Id and, more importantly, code outside of the module cannot create a new Id value without using Id::get. This enforces the assumption use_id makes about new IDs being distinct from any existing IDs. While duplicate IDs can exist, the Id type is Copy after all – Id::get will never produce a value that compares equal to any existing Id value.

Wrapping primitive types like usize and u8 to enforce the assumptions your code makes is a common pattern. While we saw one application removing the "numberness" from a usize, another wrapper type may prevent mixing values of different units.

```
#[derive(Copy, Clone, PartialEq)]
struct Rad(f32);
#[derive(Copy, Clone, PartialEq)]
struct Deg(f32);

impl From<Rad> for Deg {
  fn from(r: Rad) -> Deg {
    use std::f32::consts::PI;
    Deg(r.0 * (180.0 / PI))
  }
}

impl From<Deg> for Rad {
  fn from(f: Deg) -> Rad {
    use std::f32::consts::PI;
    Rad(f.0 * (PI / 180.0))
  }
}

fn sin(r: Rad) -> f32 { ... }
```

Here, we have a Rad type (for radians) and a Deg type (for degrees). The sin function only takes radians, which is reflected in the type signature. Mixing up the units your angles are represented in is prevented at compile time by the language.

## Extension Traits

So far, we have only discussed extending or altering types. Here, we will cover extending existing traits using a pattern known as "Extension Traits". Extension traits look a little like this:

```
use std::io;
trait WriteInt {
  fn write_i32(&mut self, i: i32) -> io::Result<()>;
}

impl<W: ?Sized + io::Write> WriteInt for W {
  fn write_i32(&mut self, i: i32) -> io::Result<()>{
    let mut buf: [u8; 4] = [0; 4];
    buf[0] = (i & 0xFF) as u8;
    buf[1] = ((i >> 8) & 0xFF) as u8;
    buf[2] = ((i >> 16) & 0xFF) as u8;
    buf[3] = ((i >> 24) & 0xFF) as u8;

    try!(self.write(&buf));
    Ok(())
  }
}

fn test() -> io::Result<()> {
  let mut csr = io::Cursor::new(vec![]);
  csr.write_i32(0x12345678)
}
```

Here, we define a new trait, WriteInt. This is our extension trait. It extends the standard-library Write trait, adding in a method for writing i32 values in little-endian format. Then, we create a "blanket implementation" of our new trait for all types that implement the Write trait. Since we do not need Self to be Sized in our implementation, we also make sure to include ?Sized to remove the implicit bound.

All extension traits follow this basic pattern – defining a trait, then implementing it on a type parameter bounded by the trait you want to extend.

The only restriction is that the blanket implementation must be the only implementation of the extension trait[1].

## Extending Local Types

So far we have focused on extending foreign types and traits. This is because local types and traits are under your control and can be altered in any way you need. However, the patterns presented here can sometimes be useful when applied to local types. Consider the following code:

```
struct File { ... }

impl File {
  fn name(&self) -> String { ... }
  fn size(&self) -> usize { ... }

  #[cfg(unix)]
  fn mode(&self) -> u16 { ... }
}
```

Here, we have a minimal representation of a file. It has methods for getting the file's name and size, and also for getting the "mode". The mode is a bitwise representation of the permissions on the file used on unix platforms. Since it is only usable on unix platforms, we use conditional compilation to only define the method on unix platforms.

In terms of preventing errors, this code works fine. Trying to call `mode` on a non-unix platform will cause the compiler to raise an error. However, it will only raise that error once you try compiling for a non-unix platform. If you are trying to write cross-platform software, you may want to know about this earlier.

The way to do this is to separate the platform-specific code into a separate trait and then implement that conditionally:

```
pub trait FileExt {
  fn mode(&self) -> u16;
}
```

1 At the time of this writing. There is a proposal for a feature called "specialization" that would relax this restriction.

```
#[cfg(unix)]
impl FileExt for File {
  fn mode(&self) -> u16 { ... }
}
```

This works because in order to call trait methods, the trait has to be in scope. Calling the platform-specific methods now requires explicit opt-in:

```
// Explicitly importing FileExt
use fs::FileExt;

fn foobar(file: &fs::File) {
  println!("{}", file.mode());
}
```

Without `use fs::FileExt`, the above code would fail to compile. It will also fail to compile on non-unix systems, as the trait would not be implemented. Having to explicitly import the trait signals that you are now using platform-specific code – something that may not have been obvious with the original code.

## KEY TAKEAWAYS

- Traits can be used to add new functionality to existing types.
- Wrapper types can be used to create distinct types to allow traits to be effectively re-implemented for a type.
- Extension traits can be used to give new functionality to all types that implement the trait being extended.

# 5

# Ownership, Borrowing & Lifetimes

Ownership, borrowing and lifetimes form the foundation of Rust semantics. Any serious use of Rust will require a good understanding of all three concepts, and none of the concepts can be properly understood without the other two. This chapter will first cover ownership, then borrowing, and finally lifetimes.

## OWNERSHIP

A typical program will often create and use many resources. Memory is one such resource – in fact, it is likely the most common resource used by a program. Despite the large amount of memory available on modern machines, however, it is still important to keep memory usage low. This entails freeing memory when it is no longer being used.

Manual memory management is a programming methodology where the programmer is responsible for allocating and, more importantly, freeing memory by manually inserting calls to the allocation and freeing functions. This is very fast and flexible. However, it can be tricky to get manual memory management correct; manual memory management can quickly get complex.

The main question to answer when doing manual memory management is, "Where has this memory been freed?". Memory can only be freed once, so we want to avoid attempting to free the same memory multiple times. We also want to make sure that it is freed somewhere, otherwise the memory will be *leaked*. A *memory leak* is a section of memory that is no longer accessible by the program but it has not been freed back to the system for reuse.

A useful tool when answering this question is the concept of ownership. Ownership allows us to say that memory is freed by its owner. This turns our original question from, "Where has the memory been freed?" to a different question, "Who owns this memory?"

## Ownership in Rust

Ownership in Rust is described by the following four (4) rules:

1. Variables own the value they represent.
2. Composite types own the values they contain.
3. Values are cleaned up (memory freed, files closed) when the owner becomes inaccessible.
4. Values have exactly one owner.

The first two rules allow us to answer the question of "Who owns this memory?" For example:

```
struct Foo {
  a: Vec<i32>,
  b: usize
}

fn bar(foo: Foo) { /***/ }
```

The `foo` variable owns a `Foo` value, which in turn owns a `Vec<i32>` and a `usize`.

The third rule tells us when memory is freed. There are two main ways a value becomes inaccessible: it is either overwritten or goes out of scope.

```
fn foo() {
  let mut v: Vec<i32> = Vec::new(); // v1
  v = vec![1,2,3]; // v2
}
```

The value v1 originally stored in v is made inaccessible when the new vector v2 is assigned to the variable. The only way to access the value v1 was through v and now v contains a different value. Finally, the v variable itself becomes inaccessible at the end of the function and the value v2 becomes inaccessible when v goes out of scope. You cannot access the v variable from outside the function.

The final rule ensures that a value is only cleaned up once. Since a value only has a single owner and the owner is responsible for cleaning it up, it follows that the value will only be cleaned up once.

Taken together, the four rules allow the compiler to insert the calls to the allocation and freeing functions for memory itself. This is similar to manual memory management, but it is the compiler performing the job, rather than a programmer.

## Moving and Copying

Enforcing the fourth rule requires a feature that is uncommon in other languages – move semantics. Move semantics refers to when an owned value is "moved" instead of copied to a new location. For large objects, moving an object between locations is much faster than copying the object between locations, so move semantics are more efficient. In Rust, this happens when ownership must be transferred from one place to another. Other systems programming languages typically stick to copy semantics and require the programmer to manually distinguish between copies and moves since those languages do not have Rust's robust ownership concepts deeply embedded in the language.

```
fn moving(v: Vec<i32>) -> Vec<i32> {
  let mut x = v;
  x.push(10);
  x
}
```

There are two moves happening here. The first is the move of the vector from v to x. The second move is the return of x from the function. Moving in Rust marks the original location as invalid, so the compiler knows that the original location no longer contains a value. We say that ownership has transferred from v to x.

However, not all types own the data they reference. Borrowed pointers, `&T` and `&mut T`, do not own the data they reference. This means that you cannot move the data out of the borrowed pointers. It is only possible to move data from the owner. If you do need ownership, you can copy the data instead.

The most common way to copy is using the `Clone` trait which provides a `clone` method that produces a full copy of the value.

```
fn clone_vec(v: &Vec<i32>) -> Vec<i32> {
  v.clone()
}
```

The entire contents of `v` are copied by the `clone` method, making it more expensive than a move. If you need ownership of a borrowed value, then it is necessary to pay the cost to do the clone.

Finally, there are `Copy` types. `Copy` types are types that implement the `Copy` trait. These are types that can be automatically copied by the compiler without requiring a call to the `clone` method. This is because the compiler performs a simple copy of the underlying memory without any special considerations for the contents of the memory.

The `Copy` trait can only be implemented on types that contain only `Copy` types. The built-in types that implement `Copy` are:

- Primitive Integers: `i8`, `i16`, `i32`, `i64`, `isize`, `u8`, `u16`, `u32`, `u64`, and `usize`.
- Floating point numbers: `f32` and `f64`.
- Booleans.
- Characters.
- Function pointers.
- Immutable borrowed pointers: `&T`.
- Raw pointers: `*const T` and `*mut T`.
- Empty tuple: `()`.
- Slices and tuples if their contained values also implement `Copy`.

# BORROWING

To understand borrowing, let's see what Rust looks like without it.

```
fn quicksort(list: Vec<i32>) -> Vec<i32> {
  if list.len() <= 1 {
    return list;
  } else if list.len() == 2 {
    if list[0] > list[1] {
      return vec![list[1], list[0]];
    } else {
      return list;
    }
  }

  let mut left = Vec::new();
  let mut right = Vec::new();

  let pivot = list[0];

  for el in &list[1..] {
    if *el <= pivot {
      left.push(*el);
    } else {
      right.push(*el);
    }
  }


  let mut left = quicksort(left);
  let right = quicksort(right);

  left.push(pivot);
  left.extend(right);

  left
}
```

This is a simple implementation of the *quicksort* algorithm. A brief description of the algorithm is this:

1. Pick an element (called a pivot) from the list.
2. Partition the list into two sub-lists where all the elements in one list are less than or equal to the pivot and all the elements in the other list are greater than the pivot.
3. Recursively sort the two sub-lists.

The implementation uses almost no borrowing; instead, almost everything is moved or copied. This means that the algorithm is slower than necessary and uses more memory than necessary. This is because we need to create new lists for partitioning and then copy one list into the other for concatenation.

The requirement of ownership for accessing data is a major inconvenience. It forces us to copy data just so that something else can read the data without us having to transfer ownership to it. For a language that wants performance, this is a problem.

Borrowing is the solution to that problem. Borrowing allows you access to some data without having to take ownership of it. There are two ways to borrow a variable: mutably and immutably. A mutable borrow allows the borrowing code to read and modify the data while an immutable borrow allows only read access to the data. The following table shows the different ways in which a variable can be accessed and what it means from an ownership perspective.

| Borrow Kind | Move | Write | Read |
|---|---|---|---|
| No Borrow (Move) | Yes | Yes | Yes |
| Mutable Borrow | No | Yes | Yes |
| Immutable Borrow | No | No | Yes |

Borrows are done using borrowed pointers. A mutable borrow uses a `&mut T` pointer and an immutable one uses a `&T` pointer. Borrowed pointers have a few rules to make sure they are safe:

1. A mutable borrow must be the only borrow of the value.

```
fn example() {
  let mut foo: Vec<i32> = vec![1,2,3];
  let foo_mut: &mut Vec<i32> = &mut foo;
  // error: cannot borrow 'foo' as immutable
  // because it is also borrowed as mutable
  let foo_ref: &Vec<i32> = &foo;
}
```

2. Borrowing something contained in a value prevents the borrowing of the complete value mutably. Likewise, if the complete value is borrowed, a contained value cannot be borrowed mutably.

```
fn example() {
  let mut foo: (i32, f32) = (1, 2.0);
  // Borrow the first field
  let i: &i32 = &foo.0;
  // error: cannot borrow 'foo' as mutable
  // because 'foo.0' is also borrowed as
  // immutable
  let foo_mut: &mut (i32, f32) = &mut foo;
}
```

3. You cannot move a value while it is borrowed.

```
fn example() {
  let foo: Vec<i32> = vec![1,2,3];
  let foo_ref: &Vec<i32> = &foo;
  // error: cannot move out of 'foo'
  // because it is borrowed
  let bar = foo;
}
```

4. You cannot assign to a variable that has been borrowed from.

```
fn example() {
  let mut foo: (i32, f32) = (1, 2.0);
  // Borrow the first field
  let i: &i32 = &foo.0;
  // error: cannot assign to 'foo'
  // because it is borrowed
  foo = (2, 1.0);
}
```

All four rules are required for safety. The most important one is the first, however, as it ensures that our code has a consistent view of the data at all times. Consider the following function:

```
fn foo(x: &mut Vec<i32>) {
  x.clear();
}
```

The `clear` method empties the `Vec`. This means that any references to the elements in the `Vec` are now invalid. When those elements are invalidated, the memory associated with them will be released for reuse. How is this safe? Looking at the signature, we see that we take the `Vec` as `&mut Vec<i32>`. By rule number one, no other section of code can have a reference to that `Vec`. By rule number two, no other section of code can have a reference to any element of the contents *because* we have that mutable reference to the `Vec`. We do not need to check other functions to know that `foo` is safe as the caller could not legally construct the reference otherwise.

Rust takes advantage of this and only carries out local checking of functions. This has consequences for the language, as we will see later, but it makes compiling Rust code much easier. Functions and methods only consider the signatures of any functions they call.

Now that we understand the rules of borrowing, let us take a fresh look at our *quicksort* function and try and improve it by making use of borrowing.

*Quicksort* can be implemented as an in-place algorithm, meaning that it can be performed by modifying the list to be sorted. This is the first change to make to our implementation:

```
fn quicksort(list: &mut [i32]) { /***/ }
```

We need to modify the list but do not need to own it, so, instead of using a `Vec`, we can use a mutable slice. Similarly, as we are no longer taking ownership, we do not need to return a sorted list; the list will simply be sorted in-place.

The first part of the function is largely the same, with a few minor alterations:

```
if list.len() <= 1 {
  return;
} else if list.len() == 2 {
  if list[0] > list[1] {
    list.swap(0, 1);
  }
  return;
}
```

We still check for zero-, one-, and two-element lists as base cases for the sort. The two-element case is interesting, though, as we use the `swap` method on the list to swap the two elements around. We will see that method again shortly.

Selecting the pivot element is entirely unchanged, so instead we will look at partitioning. This code requires significant changes compared to the original, as we are no longer using two new lists to partition into. Instead, we swap elements around:

```
let mut i = 0;
for j in 0..list.len() {
  if list[j] < pivot {
    list.swap(i, j);
    i += 1;
  }
}

let (left, right) = list.split_at_mut(i);
```

This swaps any element greater than the pivot to the beginning of the list. Once it gets to the end of the list, `i` is the position where all elements before it are less than the pivot and all elements above are greater than the pivot. The last line of this section is the interesting part, though, as we use the method `split_at_mut` to get two mutable slices into the list. To understand why we need to use this method, let us look at the naïve way of creating the two slices:

```
let left = &mut list[..i];
let right = &mut list[i..];
```

This seems like it should work but it violates the rule that there must only be a single mutable borrow around at a time. While we are borrowing non-overlapping sections of the list, we also borrow the `list` mutably in both cases, triggering an error. The `split_at_mut` method uses unsafe code behind the scenes to allow the creation of two mutable references to the same list, while manually enforcing that the mutable slices returned do not overlap. You can find more details about this in Chapter 13.

The final part of our revised function recursively sorts our sublists:

```
quicksort(left);
quicksort(right);
```

Since sorting is now done in-place, we no longer need to reconstruct a single list from the two parts. The full function, making use of borrowing, is this:

```
pub fn quicksort(list: &mut [i32]) {
    if list.len() <= 1 {
        return;
    } else if list.len() == 2 {
        if list[0] > list[1] {
            list.swap(0, 1);
        }
        return;
    }

    let pivot = list[0];

    let mut i = 0;
    for j in 0..list.len() {
        if list[j] < pivot {
            list.swap(i, j);
            i += 1;
        }
    }

    let (left, right) = list.split_at_mut(i);

    quicksort(left);
    quicksort(right);
}
```

Where the original version allocated two new vectors in most calls, this one does no allocation at all. In fact, very little extra memory is used at all, just the small amount of stack space required to store the sub-slices as we recurse. By keeping the amount of memory allocated low, we can improve the run-time efficiency of our algorithm since extra allocations and copies do not have to occur during the execution of the sort. Being able to minimize the memory usage and run-time speed of the algorithm, while still programming in a safe manner, is one of the main advantages that Rust provides over other programming languages.

## LIFETIMES

Borrowing is a powerful tool used for both safety and performance since it allows Rust to enforce the single ownership of a piece of data while still allowing the data to be safely shared between functions and data structures. However, there is a major limitation associated with borrowing. Take a look at the following code (ignore the 'a business, we will get to that shortly):

```
fn fail_example<'a>() -> &'a [i32] {
  let y = [1,2,3];
  let ret: &[i32] = &y[..];
  ret
}
```

Looking at the types involved, this looks like it should work. After all, ret has the type &[i32] and the function says that it returns an &[i32]. Everything matches up. The problem is that we are taking a reference to y, and y goes out of scope when the function returns. The returned reference points to a dropped value!

Fortunately, Rust knows this is a bad idea and gives you this error:

```
error: 'y' does not live long enough
```

It knows that y only lives for the body of the function, so a reference to y will not be valid after the function returns. As the reference stored in ret is returned, it lives longer than y, which is not allowed. This leads us to the central rule of lifetimes in Rust:

> A reference must not out-live the data it references.

Lifetimes exist to allow this rule to be followed while increasing the safety and flexibility of references. Everything about lifetimes is built on top of this rule.

## What are Lifetimes?

Before we can talk about the lifetime system itself, we need to get a handle on what a lifetime is. One definition is this:

> A lifetime is the length of time a variable lives.

This definition is simple and hides a lot of detail, but it is accurate. How long a variable lives is most often the scope it was defined in. Take the following example:

```
fn example(x: Vec<i32>) {
  let y = x[0];
  {
    let z = if y > 0 {
      let w1 = x[1];
      w1
    } else {
      let w2 = x[2];
      w2
    };
  }

}
```

Each line indicates where the matching variable starts and ends – they are the variable's lifetime. x is an argument, so it starts just before the function body and dies right at the end. Every other variable starts where it was defined and ends where the enclosing scope finishes.

Now, you may be wondering how this part works:

```
let z = if y > 0 {
  let w1 = x[1];
  w1
} else {
  let w2 = x[2];
  w2
}
```

If w1 and w2 are confined to the scope they were defined in, how does the assignment to z work? This is due to an important distinction between *variables* and *values*.

While a variable cannot exist outside of its lifetime, a value can be passed around for as long it is valid. Since an `i32` value is always valid, we can assign the value `w1` or `w2` contains to `z`. How long a value is valid for is called its *lifetime bound* and, like variables, values cannot exist outside of that bound.

Let us take another look at our failing code from earlier:

```
1  fn fail_example<'a>() -> &'a [i32] {
2    let y = [1,2,3];
3    let ret: &[i32] = &y[..];
4    ret
5  }
```

Now that we have talked a little about lifetimes, let us work through why this is invalid.

First, let us look at the lifetimes involved. We have two variables, `y` and `ret`:

| Variable | Variable Lifetime | Type | Value Lifetime |
|---|---|---|---|
| y | Line 2 – Line 4 | `[i32; 3]` | `'static` |
| ret | Line 3 – Line 4 | `&[i32]` | `'$y` |

This table shows the two variables' lifetimes, types and the lifetime bounds of the values they contain. The `'static` lifetime is a special lifetime that represents the lifetime of the entire program. The `'static` lifetime is longer than every other lifetime and, as a lifetime bound, indicates that the value is always valid. The `'$y` lifetime is not valid Rust syntax, but instead represents the lifetime of the `y` variable for the purposes of this table. Valid lifetime syntax includes the `'` mark followed by an identifier. Many times, lifetime identifiers are short identifiers because they are very generic. So, you typically see lifetimes like `'a`, `'b`, or `'c`. However, you can be more descriptive in your lifetime identifiers, if you like.

Remember that our core rule is that references must not outlive the entity they reference. The reference inside the `ret` variable is a reference to the `y` variable, and therefore has a lifetime bound equal to the lifetime of `y`.

Returning the reference means that the value must outlive the lifetime of the function body itself since the value continues existing after the function call. However, the '$y lifetime ends inside the function and any references to it must not outlive it. These conflicting constraints result in the error message we saw before.

## Lifetime Parameters on Functions

Here is the function signature for fail_example again:

```
fn fail_example<'a>() -> &'a [i32];
```

The 'a syntax represents a lifetime parameter. It appears in the type parameter list because lifetimes work similarly to type parameters. Instead of representing an unknown type, it represents an unknown lifetime.

```
fn get<T>(slice: &[T], idx: usize) -> T;
```

The T in get is a type parameter, meaning that it can be any type. However, T means the same thing in all the places it is used in the function signature, so we know that if we pass in a &[i8], for example, we will get an i8 in return.

Inside the function, we only know what the bounds on T say. Extending the get function a little, we can write this:

```
fn get<T: Clone>(slice: &[T], idx: usize) -> T {
  slice[idx].clone()
}
```

We know we can call clone because the bounds on T say that it must implement Clone. However, we cannot know if T is an i8, or a String or any specific type.

Getting back to lifetime parameters, they mean the same thing.

```
fn get<'a, T>(slice: &'a [T], idx: usize) -> &'a T;
```

This version of get returns a reference. In &'a T, 'a refers to the lifetime bound of the reference itself. Like with type parameters, the 'a lifetime refers to the same lifetime in all places it is used in the function signature.

```
1 fn main() {
2   let a = [1, 2, 3, 4];
3   let s = &a[..];
4
5   let item = get(s, 2);
6 }
```

Let us now build another table of variables like before. This time, we have three variables – `a`, `s` and `item`.

| Variable | Lifetime | Type | Value Lifetime |
|---|---|---|---|
| `a` | Line 2 – Line 5 | `[i32; 4]` | `'static` |
| `s` | Line 3 – Line 5 | `&[i32]` | `'$a` |
| `item` | Line 5 – Line 5 | `&i32` | ??? |

As before, the fixed-sized array has a `'static` lifetime bound. The reference to it, in the form of the slice, has the bound `'$a`. What is the lifetime bound for the value in `item`?

We can figure this out by substituting in the generic parameters for concrete ones:

```
fn get(slice: &'$a [i32], idx: usize) -> &'$a i32;
```

We replaced the `'a` lifetime in `get` with `'$a` since all `'a`s in the signature refer to the same lifetime; we know that get returns a `&'$a i32`.

This is how lifetime parameters work for the caller, but what about the function itself:

```
fn get<'a, T>(slice: &'a [T], idx: usize) -> &'a T {
  let item = &slice[idx];
  item
}
```

As with type parameters, functions can only use the information supplied in the function signature when working with lifetimes. Unlike type parameters, however, there is one implied bound for lifetime parameters – the lifetime will always outlive the function. This means that we know that whatever lifetime gets substituted in for the 'a parameter in the get function, it will be longer than any lifetime inside of the function.

&slice[idx] takes a reference to an element of the slice with the same lifetime bound as the slice itself. Since slice is &'a [T], we know that item must contain &'a T, which matches our return type!

This is what allows references to be safely returned from a function. Since we tie together the lifetime bounds of the arguments and the return type, we can check that the returned value is used properly.

## Omitting Lifetimes

Lifetime parameters on functions can be omitted in some circumstances. There are two cases: anonymous lifetimes and lifetime elision.

Anonymous lifetimes are those for which it is not necessary to refer to the lifetime in the function. This normally occurs because you are returning a non-reference type. For example, getting the length of a slice:

```
fn len<T>(s: &[T]) -> usize { /***/ }
```

The lifetime of the slice is not relevant to the function, so it can be omitted.

Lifetime elision refers to the ability of the compiler to figure out how the lifetimes relate in the function signature. This is most often used when there is a single lifetime in the function arguments and a single lifetime in the return type. For example, our get method from earlier could be written as:

```
fn get<T>(slice: &[T], idx: usize) -> &T { /***/ }
```

The compiler can figure out that the lifetime of the &[T] must be the same as the lifetime for the returned &T, so it does not require the lifetime to be specified.

## Lifetime Parameters on Types

Lifetime parameters on functions allow us to accept and return references safely. What if you want to store a reference, though? This is where lifetime parameters on types come in.

```
struct Foo<'a> {
  numbers: &'a [i32],
  id: usize
}
```

Again, lifetime parameters function similarly to type parameters; they represent some unknown lifetime. However, lifetime parameters impose an implicit bound on the type they parameterize – a value of this type must not outlive any of the lifetime parameters it contains.

We will further discuss types with lifetime parameters in the next section.

## Lifetime Bounds

So far, we have discussed lifetime bounds as a restriction on how long a value is allowed to exist. In all the cases so far, the bounds have been implicit, as they must always be in place for the code to be correct, so Rust does not force you to add them manually.

However, sometimes lifetime bounds *do* need to be added manually. There are three (3) kinds of lifetime bounds: bounds on type parameters, bounds on lifetime parameters, and bounds on trait objects.

```
struct Ref<'a, T: 'a> {
  refer: &'a T
}
```

This struct has a lifetime parameter, `'a`, and a type parameter, `T`. The type parameter is bounded by `'a` using the syntax `T: 'a`. Lifetime bounds can be read as "`T` is valid for at least as long as the lifetime `'a`".

Bounds on lifetime parameters are similar:

```
struct Strings<'l, 's: 'l> {
  list: &'l [&'s str]
}
```

This struct has two lifetime parameters, `'l` and `'s`. The second lifetime, `'s`, is bounded by the lifetime `'l` using the same syntax as for type parameters: `'s: 'l`. This can similarly be read as "`'s` is valid for at least as long as `'l`".

These bounds are required so that Rust does not have to inspect the type to determine these bounds. Everything Rust needs to know about the type is available in the type signature.

The third kind of bound – bounds on trait objects – are used when you need to add lifetime bound information to a trait object.

```
trait Object {
  fn name<'a>(&'a self) -> &'a str;
}

struct Person<'s> {
  name: &'s str,
  age: u32
}
impl<'s> Object for Person<'s> {
  fn name<'a>(&'a self) -> &'a str {
    self.name
  }
}

fn make_person_object<'s>(
    name: &'s str, age: u32) -> Box<Object + 's> {
  let person = Person {
    name: name,
    age: age
  };

  let person: Box<Person<'s>> = Box::new(person);

  person
}
```

make_person_object returns a boxed trait object of Object. However, the trait has a bound of 's, which is the same as the lifetime of the name string. To understand why it is required here, let us look at what happens when we remove the + 's (using Rust 1.15.1):

```
error: the type 'Person<'s>' does not fulfill the required lifetime
note: type must outlive the static lifetime
```

At the end of the function, where we are returning our Person object, Rust is attempting to turn Box<Person<'s>> into Box<Object>. However, Box<Object> has an implicit 'static bound, like this: Box<Object + 'static>. Since Person<'s> does not satisfy the 'static bound, we get an error.

The explicit bound is required because trait objects throw away type information to allow the decision about which specific object is hidden behind the trait object to be made at run-time. This includes information about lifetimes, such as the lifetime parameter on `Person`. This is unsafe, as it would allow the reference `Person` contains to outlive its lifetime. To handle this, you must add the lifetime information back into the trait object using a lifetime bound.

## KEY TAKEAWAYS

- Rust moves values between variables by default, freeing memory when the final owner goes out of scope.
- You can instead "borrow" the contents of a variable, but you are limited to one mutable borrow of a variable at a time or any number of immutable borrows.
- The lifetime of a variable defines how long the variable exists in scope. The lifetime of a value defines how long the value is valid (before it goes inaccessible and will be freed).
- Lifetime parameters on function or types act like type parameters. They are generic values that are substituted in when the function or type instance is instantiated.

6

# Iterators

## INTRODUCTION

Let us take a look at iterators – a powerful feature in Rust. Iterators are an abstraction over the concept of generically traversing items, often in some sort of container. When you think "generically" in Rust, your mind should immediately go to Traits. Rust implements the iterator abstraction as a trait so that you can write generic functions that work for all iterators. To assist you in writing generic functions with iterators, the Iterator trait provides a slew of adapter functions that you can compose together to build arbitrarily complex functions that are quick and efficient.

The Iterator trait is designed for performance and usability, so iterators are used almost everywhere in Rust. You will find iterators crop up when you want to walk across all of the items in a `Vec` or in a `HashMap`. However, iterators are not restricted to traversing containers; Rust also provides iterators over the lines in a file, the arguments in a command line, and random numbers generated by a random number generator. The following example shows one of the simplest uses of iterators:

```
fn main() {
    for i in 1..6 {
        println!("i == {:?}", i);
    }
}
```

Which prints the following:

```
i == 1
i == 2
i == 3
i == 4
i == 5
```

Now, you might be thinking, so, iterators are a replacement for a `for` loop in C? Well, yes, iterators in this form can be used as a `for` loop replacement, but iterators are more general than this simple example. In general, an iterator represents a sequence of values that can be operated on. More precisely, an iterator is a type that you can call `next` on to get the `next` element in the sequence represented by the iterator. The previous example is equivalent to this:

```
fn main() {
    let mut r = 1..6;
    loop {
        match r.next() {
            Some(i) => {
                println!("i == {:?}", i);
            }
            None => { break; }
        }
    }
}
```

In both examples, the range syntax of `1..6` produces an iterator of the sequence of values from 1 to 6. The `next` method returns an `Option`, with `None` indicating the end of the sequence provided by the iterator. You might notice that we made a mutable binding to `r`, this is because the `next` method actually modifies `r` so it knows which number to return next. The requirement for having a `next` method is provided by the `Iterator` trait. All iterators implement this trait.

Ranges are one of simplest iterators around, so let us take a look at something a little more complex.

```
fn main() {
    let v = vec![1,2,3,4,5];

    for &i in v.iter() {
        println!("i == {:?}", i);
    }
}
```

This example iterates over a `Vec<i32>` and does a few things that the previous examples do not. First, we are using `v.iter()` instead of using `v` directly. In this example, `v` is a `Vec<i32>` and does not implement the `Iterator` trait. However, it does provide the `v.iter()` method that returns a new type that implements `Iterator` instead. So, we would say that `v` is a sequence of `i32` values, but the type returned by `v.iter()` is an iterator that returns each value in turn from the sequence `v`.

The second thing this example does differently than the previous one is that it uses `&i` instead of just `i`. This is because `for` loops take on a pattern and not just a single variable, allowing you to unpack the element produced by the iterator. The iterator produced by `v.iter()` actually produces references to the elements in `v` so we use the `&i` pattern to extract the number from the reference.

The basic concept to remember about iterators is that they produce all of the values in a sequence, with one value being produced every time the `next` method is called on the iterator. But, what would you do if you wanted to skip values in the sequence or perform some operation on the values of the sequence? This is where iterator adapters come into play.

## ITERATOR ADAPTERS

The iterators we have seen so far are what we like to call "base" iterators. They are the iterators that directly produce the values in a sequence. However, there is a second class of iterator known as iterator adapters that are used to modify the results of another iterator. Rust provides a wide array of iterator adapters that are used to package common functionality that you might want to do to a sequence of values. These pieces of functionality are named so that they add greater semantic value to your programs. That is, by naming these common routines, it makes it easier to read a program and understand what is going on with it once you know what the names mean.

The following example uses the `Map` iterator adapter, constructed using the `map` method that is available on all iterators. `Map` takes each element of the original iterator and applies the function you pass to it. In this case, the function adds 1 to each element. The semantic information that the `Map` adapter adds is "this function is applied to every value in the sequence".

```
fn main() {

       let v = vec![1,2,3,4,5];

       for i in v.iter().map(|&i| i + 1) {
           println!("i == {:?}", i);
       }
}
```

Which prints:

```
i == 2
i == 3
i == 4
i == 5
i == 6
```

Often, we will talk about mapping a function over an iterator. The term "mapping" comes from mathematics and refers to a visual mapping diagram that shows how the input relates to the output of a function. In the example, our mapping function that adds 1 to the input looks like Figure 6-1.

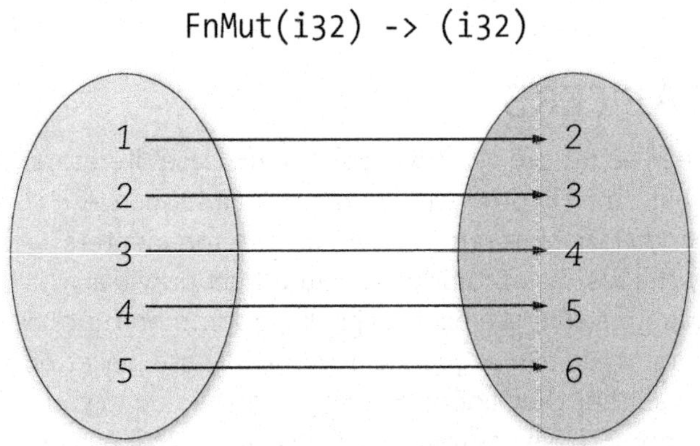


**Figure 6-1:** Mapping a function over an iterator

One of the strengths of iterators in general, and especially iterator adapters, is that they are "lazy". To be lazy means that the iterator adapters do not do any work until you ask for the next element. This makes them much more efficient than constructing another list of elements to hold intermediate results. So, in the case of the Map iterator adapter, a whole new list of elements is not being created to hold the incremented value. Instead, for each cycle through the for loop, the for loop syntax asks for a value from the Map iterator using next, which calls down to the Vec<i32> iterator to get the value. The Map iterator then calls the incrementing function on it and returns it from its own next call.

Another common operation to do on a sequence of values is to be able to enumerate, or uniquely name, each item in the sequence. Rust provides another built-in iterator adapter to do just that, the Enumerate adapter:

```
fn main() {
    let v = vec![1,2,3,4,5];

    for (i, val) in v.iter().enumerate() {
        println!("v[{}] == {:?}", i, val);
    }
}
```

Output:

```
v[0] == 1
v[1] == 2
v[2] == 3
v[3] == 4
v[4] == 5
```

Enumerate takes an iterator and returns a new one that produces a tuple containing a counter and the original value. For the example above, the counter is the index of the vector, but you can use enumerate on any iterator, so it is not always an index. The semantic value that the Enumerate adapter adds is, "this associates a monotonically increasing number with each element in the sequence."

Often, you do not actually need every element in the sequence. The Filter iterator is used to remove elements from the sequence:

```
fn main() {
    let v = vec![1,2,3,4,5,6];

    for i in v.iter().filter(|&i| (i % 2) == 0) {
        println!("i == {:?}", i);
    }
}
```

This outputs:

```
i == 2
i == 4
i == 6
```

The `Filter` adapter takes a predicate function[1] that is evaluated on the value provided by the underlying iterator. If the predicate returns `false` for the value, the `Filter` adapter skips over the elements. The function in the example tests for even numbers and, as you can see, only the even numbers are printed. The semantic value that the `Filter` adapter adds is "this function is used to decide whether or not to keep each element in the sequence."

Each of the iterator adapters that we have mentioned, and all iterator adapters in general, wrap up another iterator and adapt it to provide the new functionality. This is great since it lets us arbitrarily chain the iterators together, building up more and more complex iterator chains out of simpler, basic components. But what do we mean by simpler, basic components? In all of the examples we have seen thus far, the function passed to the iterator adapter was a simple, anonymous function. However, we can pass reusable, named functions as well. We could define the following functions for working with the `Map` and `Filter` adapters:

```
fn addOne(v: &i32) -> i32 {
    v + 1
}

fn even(v: &&i32) -> bool {
    (*v % 2) == 0
}

fn main() {
    let v = vec![1,2,3,4,5,6];

    for i in v.iter()
             .filter(even)
             .map(addOne) {
        println!("i == {:?}", i);
    }
}
```

---

1 A predicate function is a function from some value to a boolean result. It is typically used to determine whether a value belongs to a particular class. For instance, the predicate even would be a function `Fn(&&i32) -> bool` that returns true when the argument is even and false when the argument is odd.

Where iterators are an abstraction over traversing a collection, iterator adapters are a set of named abstractions of specific ways of traversing a collection. By chaining iterator adapters together, we are able to build more complex programs from simple components, making it easier to read and reason out the code that we are writing. For instance, you can understand or test the `even` function or the `addOne` function, independent of the rest of the iterator chain. Then, if you see those functions used in other places or as part of other iterator chains, you do not have to figure out what they mean all over again. Contrast this to a plain for loop that just open-coded all of the conditional logic right in the loop body. In that case, you would have to figure out what that loop did by really scrutinizing the code every time you saw a loop expressed that way. The ability to abstract over loops is the power that the iterator-chaining ability that Rust provides. The following example shows another simple iterator chain:

```
fn main() {
    let v = vec![1,2,3,4,5,6,7,8];

    let iter = v.iter()
        .enumerate()
        .map(|(i, &v)| (i, (v as f32) / 3.0))
        .filter(|&(_, v)| v > 1.0);
    for (i, val) in iter {
        println!("v[{}] == {:?}", i, val);
    }
}
```

Output:

```
v[3] == 1.3333334
v[4] == 1.6666666
v[5] == 2
v[6] == 2.3333333
v[7] == 2.6666667
```

This uses the three adapters we have discussed so far to build a more complex iterator. Iterator chains work by calling `next` on the inner iterator and then applying the appropriate modification. In this instance, Filter calls into the Map iterator which then calls into the Enumerate iterator which finally gets the next value from the vector's iterator. Going back up the chain, `Enumerate` wraps the value in a tuple and adds the counter. `Map` then applies the function to that tuple and then `Filter` skips over values where the function returns false. In Figure 6-2 we can see how the values change as each iterator adapter is applied in turn.

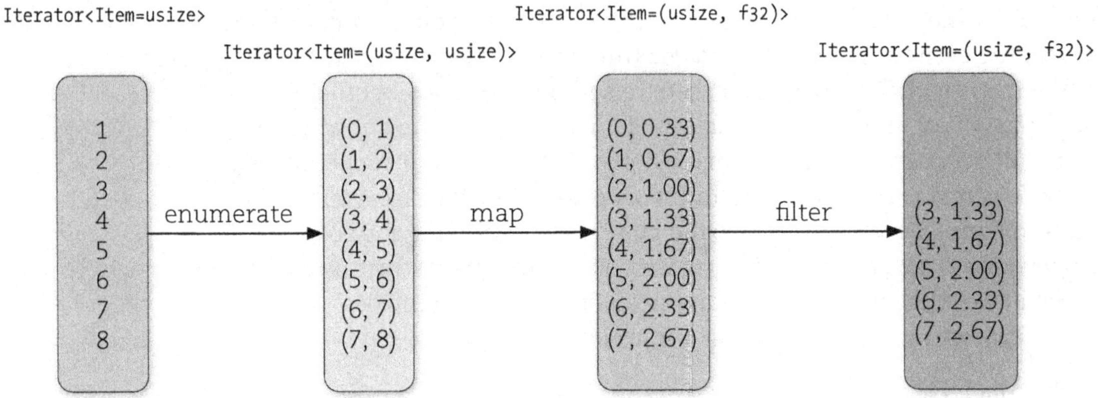


**Figure 6-2:** Iterator adapter chain

Chains like these can be as long as you want and use many other adapters, like `FilterMap`, which combine the functionality of `Filter` and `Map`, `Zip` – which allows you to iterate over two iterators at once – and `Chain` – which allows you chain two iterators together. Once you have built up an iterator chain, you can use the produced iterator in a `for` loop to retrieve all of the values that the iterator chain will produce. Producing values with a `for` loop seems very manual, though. Everything we have seen regarding iterators thus far points to using functional abstraction to make it easier to reuse software components or to make it easier to reason out the code. What if there was a functional way to abstract across consuming all of the values in the iterator? The good news is, there is a way with the consumer methods found on iterators.

## CONSUMERS

There are a number of special methods on iterators that "consume" the iterator. This means that they run through the iterator to produce their return value. Some consume the entire iterator, while others may only consume some of them.

The most common consumer is the `collect` method. `collect` uses the iterator to construct a new collection, most often used to construct new `Vec<T>`s.

```
fn main() {
    let v: Vec<i32> = (0..10).collect();
    println!("{:?}", v);
}
```

The `collect` in this example is called on a `Range` iterator to produce a vector that contains ten elements counting from zero.

The `collect` method can also be used to construct other collections than just vectors:

```
use std::collections::HashMap;
fn main() {
    let chars = ['a', 'b', 'c'];
    let s: String = chars.iter().cloned().collect();
    println!("{:?}", s);

    let v = vec![("a", 1), ("b", 2)];
    let map: HashMap<_, _> = v.iter()
        .cloned().collect();
    println!("{:?}", map);
}
```

The first portion of the example uses `collect` to construct a new `String` from an iterator over `chars`. It also introduces a new iterator adapter, the `Cloned` adapter, which clones borrowed values to produce owned values; that is, it maps from `&T` to `T`. The second portion of the example constructs a `HashMap` from an iterator over pairs of `(key, value)`.

Another useful consumer is `nth` which provides basic indexing on iterators. `nth` consumes the iterator until it gets to the index you want or the iterator is empty. In the following example, we will grab the element at the 1-index in the iterator (`nth` starts its count as 0), so we will print out the character 'b'.

```
fn main() {
    let chars = ['a', 'b', 'c'];
    if let Some(c) = chars.iter().nth(1) {
        println!("{:?}", c);
    }
}
```

## BUILDING YOUR OWN ITERATOR

So now we know how to use iterators and adapters. But what about building your own? This is especially important for writers of collections since collections tend to be sequences of values, but it is also useful in many other cases. For instance, you might want to define an iterator over a sequence of messages to come in over the network or over configuration values in a config file. For our example iterator, though, we will define a very simple collection to work with:

```
pub struct LinkedList<T> {
    head: Option<Node<T>>
}

struct Node<T> {
    val: T,
    next: Option<Box<Node<T>>>
}
```

This is a basic singly-linked list; each node has a value and a pointer to the next node. The iterator we will write for this collection will just traverse the list from beginning to end.

Before we start, however, we should take a look at the `Iterator` trait:

```
pub trait Iterator {
    type Item;

    fn next(&mut self) -> Option<Self::Item>;
    fn size_hint(&self) -> (usize, Option<usize>) {
        (0, None)
    }
}
```

We have already discussed the `next` method, so let us take a look at the other parts. The `type Item` is an associated type, describing the type that iterator will produce. You can see it being used in the definition of the `next` method. The other method is `size_hint`, which is used to hint at the number of elements the iterator may produce. The `size_hint` method can be used by consumers of the iterator to pre-allocate a reasonable amount of storage to hold the elements of the iterator. For example, the `collect` method might use `size_hint` to get an idea of how many elements the iterator represents. It is much more efficient to simply allocate the total size up front rather than continually bump the memory allocation up as new elements get added to a vector. `size_hint` has a default implementation that returns the most conservative range possible, namely that the lower bound is 0 and that there is no known upper bound.

Collections normally have multiple ways to iterate their contents: by immutable reference, by mutable reference and by-value. We will cover all three for our linked list.

## By Immutable Reference

To start with, we will define the iterator type itself:

```
pub struct Iter<'a, T: 'a> {
    current_node: Option<&'a Node<T>>
}
```

This contains all the state we will need to traverse the list, i.e. a reference to the "current" node that the iterator is located. If `current_node` is `None`, then we have finished traversing the list.

Next, we will implement `Iterator` for `Iter`:

```
impl<'a, T> Iterator for Iter<'a, T> {
    type Item = &'a T;

    fn next(&mut self) -> Option<&'a T> {
        if let Some(curr) = self.current_node {
            self.current_node = curr.next
                .as_ref()
                .map(|n| &**n);
            Some(&curr.val)
        } else {
            None
        }
    }
}
```

Here, we take the current node and check to see if it is `None` or `Some`. If it is `None`, we simply return `None` as we have reached the end of the list. Otherwise, we extract the `next` node from the current one and update the `current_node` field. The next node is actually `Option<Box<T>>`, and we need an `Option<&T>` to store in the `current_node` field. We do this by using the `as_ref` and `map` methods on `Option` to turn the contained `Box<T>` into a `&T`. How we get there in the map method is a bit confusing, so let us break it down a bit. We need to produce an `Option<&'a Node<T>>`, since this is the type of `current_node`.

| | |
|---|---|
| `curr.next.as_ref()` | `Option<&Box<Node<T>>>` |
| `curr.next.as_ref().map(\|n\| *n)` | `Option<Box<Node<T>>>` |
| `curr.next.as_ref().map(\|n\| **n)` | `Option<Node<T>>` |
| `curr.next.as_ref().map(\|n\| &**n)` | `Option<&Node<T>>` |

The last step to building up our iterator is to provide a way to make an `Iter` from the `LinkedList`:

```
impl<T> LinkedList<T> {
    pub fn iter<'a>(&'a self) -> Iter<'a, T> {
        let head = self.head.as_ref();
        Iter {
            current_node: head
        }
    }
}
```

This constructs an `Iter` using the `head` node as the initial node in the iterator and returns it.

## By Mutable Reference

This iterator and the by-value are very similar to the by immutable reference iterator, so we will present the entire iterator at once and discuss the differences.

```
pub struct IterMut<'a, T: 'a> {
    current_node: Option<&'a mut Node<T>>
}

impl<'a, T> Iterator for IterMut<'a, T> {
    type Item = &'a mut T;

    fn next(&mut self) -> Option<&'a mut T> {
        let curr = self.current_node.take();
```

```
        if let Some(mut curr) = curr {
            self.current_node = curr.next
                .as_mut()
                .map(|n| &mut **n);
            Some(&mut curr.val)
        } else {
            None
        }
    }
}

impl<T> LinkedList<T> {
    pub fn iter_mut<'a>(&'a mut self) -> IterMut<'a, T> {
        let head = self.head.as_mut();
        IterMut {
            current_node: head
        }
    }
}
```

As you can see, the mutable reference iterator is very similar to the immutable version. Most of the changes are from using immutable references to mutable ones. The most important difference is in the implementation of the Iterator trait. We must use take to extract the mutable reference from the current_node field. This is due to borrowing restrictions that prevent having multiple mutable references at once.

## By Value

The by value iterator actually consumes the list itself in order to work. Rather than storing a reference to a node, the iterator owns the node. Each time next is called, it removes the next node from the current one and updates current_node with it. Otherwise, the code is very similar to the other two iterators as seen below:

```
pub struct ByValueIter<T> {
    current_node: Option<Node<T>>
}

impl<T> Iterator for ByValueIter<T> {
    type Item = T;

    fn next(&mut self) -> Option<T> {
        let curr = self.current_node.take();
        if let Some(curr) = curr {
            self.current_node = curr.next
```

```
                .map(|n| *n);
            Some(curr.val)
        } else {
            None
        }
    }
}

impl<T> LinkedList<T> {
    pub fn byval_iter(self) -> ByValueIter<T> {
        let head = self.head;
        ByValueIter {
            current_node: head
        }
    }
}
```

## IntoIterator

Take a look at this code:

```
fn main() {
    let v = vec![1,2,3,4,5];

    for i in v {
        println!("i == {:?}", i);
    }
}
```

It is similar to the earlier examples but you may notice a small difference – we are not calling the `iter` method on `v`! This is because there is a second trait related to iterators at play – `IntoIterator`.

`IntoIterator` is defined as follows:

```
pub trait IntoIterator {
    type Item;
    type IntoIter: Iterator<Item=Self::Item>;

    fn into_iter(self) -> Self::IntoIter;
}
```

The `into_iter` method is used to turn the value provided to the for loop into an iterator. The following example is equivalent to the previous one:

```
fn main() {

    let v = vec![1,2,3,4,5];
```

```
    let mut iter = IntoIterator::into_iter(v);
    loop {
        match iter.next() {
            Some(i) => {
                println!("i == {:?}", i);
            }
            None => { break; }
        }
    }
}
```

IntoIterator is automatically implemented for all iterators; however, it can also be implemented for other types. There are three implementations of IntoIterator for our linked list, mirroring the three iterators we have already built.

```
impl<'a, T> IntoIterator for &'a LinkedList<T> {
    type Item = &'a T;
    type IntoIter = Iter<'a, T>;

    fn into_iter(self) -> Iter<'a, T> {
        self.iter()
    }
}

impl<'a, T> IntoIterator for &'a mut LinkedList<T> {
    type Item = &'a mut T;
    type IntoIter = IterMut<'a, T>;

    fn into_iter(self) -> IterMut<'a, T> {
        self.iter_mut()
    }
}

impl<T> IntoIterator for LinkedList<T> {
    type Item = T;
    type IntoIter = ByValueIter<T>;

    fn into_iter(self) -> ByValueIter<T> {
        let head = self.head;
        ByValueIter {
            current_node: head
        }
    }
}
```

The third implementation replaces the `byval_iter` method we defined earlier. The other two can be used in a for loop by doing `for i in &v` and `for i in &mut v` for the `Iter` and `IterMut` versions, respectively. Many collections have a similar set of implementations following the same pattern.

## BUILDING YOUR OWN ADAPTER

Finally, let us take a look at implementing a custom iterator adapter. For most tasks, the standard library adapters are sufficient. However, for the sake of completeness, let us implement a custom iterator adapter anyway. Specifically, we will implement a variant of the standard `Zip` adapter. The `Zip` adapter stops when either input iterator has finished; our adapter will produce elements until both iterators are finished.

Building an iterator adapter is similar to building a base iterator. We start with a type definition:

```
pub struct ZipLongest<I, J>
      where I: Iterator,
      J: Iterator
{
    i: I,
    j: J,
}
```

The type of our `ZipLongest` adapter is fairly simple. All we have to store are the two iterators that we will be iterating over. Next, we need to implement the `Iterator` trait for our iterator:

```
impl<I, J> Iterator for ZipLongest<I, J>
      where I: Iterator,
      J: Iterator
{
    type Item = (Option<I::Item>, Option<J::Item>);

    fn next(&mut self) -> Option<Self::Item> {
        let i = self.i.next();
        let j = self.j.next();

        if i.is_none() && j.is_none() {
            None
```

```
        } else {
            Some((i, j))
        }
    }
}
```

Our iterator produces pairs of (Option<T>, Option<U>). The next method gets the next elements from the two inner iterators, if both iterators return None, ZipLongest also returns None. Otherwise, a pair of Options is returned.

## OTHER ITERATOR TRAITS

There are a number of other standard library traits related to iterators that exist for specific purposes.

### FromIterator

FromIterator is used by collect to construct a collection from an iterator. Implementing this trait on a collection allows it to be used by collect.

### DoubleEndedIterator

DoubleEndedIterator is used for iterators that can be consumed from both ends. For example, a vector can be iterated from the end of the iterator, backwards. Implementing this trait allows for the use of some extra iterator adapters, notably the Rev adapter that reverses the iterator.

### ExactSizeIterator

ExactSizeIterator is used for iterators that can provide the exact length of the iterator. For example, a vector knows exactly how many elements are in the container and, thus, how many the iterator can provide. The ExactSizeIterator provides a len and an is_empty function to allow the consumer to efficiently walk the iterator. Implementing this trait allows for some iterator adapters and for consumers to be more efficient if they are used on ExactSizeIterator iterators, notably the Count adapter which counts the number of items produced by the iterator.

## Extend

The Extend trait can be implemented on a collection and is used to extend the collection with the contents of an iterator. It provides a single method, extend, that takes in any type that implements the IntoIterator trait and consumes the iterator. The implementer of the trait takes each value produced by the iterator and inserts the value into the collection.

# STREAMING ITERATORS

Streaming iterators (also called streams) are a special kind of iterator that addresses a limitation with Rust's basic iterators.

Recall the definition of the next method for the Iterator trait:

```
fn next(&mut self) -> Option<Self::Item>
```

Breaking down this method, it suggests that it takes a mutable reference to self and returns a value of the associated Item type. What it does not indicate, however, is a connection between the reference and the return value. This means that the lifetime of the value that the next method returns cannot be tied to the lifetime of the reference to self.

To understand what this means, let us look at an example. As streaming iterators is a more advanced pattern, we will inevitably need a more advanced example. With that in mind, we will use a fictional audio decoder that produces audio samples from a compressed file.

As show in Figure 6-3, as time passes, our audio decoder will periodically produce N-channel samples.

**Figure 6-3:** Example of an audio decoder

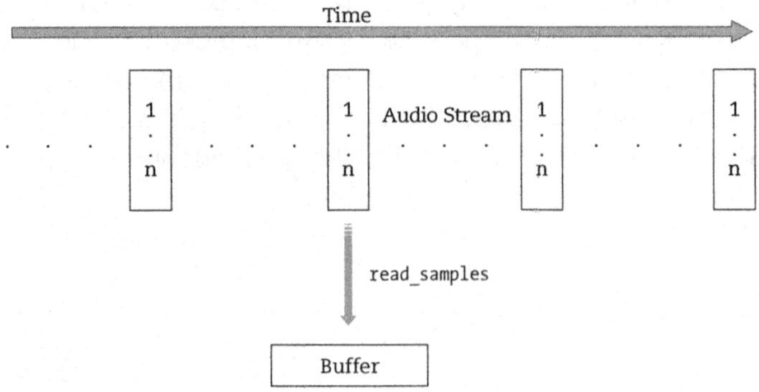

We want to be able to read those samples from the audio stream, whenever they are ready, into a buffer that we have pre-allocated. We have the following API to work with:

```
struct AudioStream { ... }

impl AudioStream {
    fn num_channels(&self) -> usize;
    fn read_samples(&mut self,
                    buffer: &mut [f32]);
    fn has_samples(&self) -> bool;
}
```

The number of channels is fixed for the entire audio stream and is returned by `num_channels`. `read_samples` reads the next set of samples from the stream and places them into `buffer`; the buffer must be large enough to hold one sample per channel, so `read_samples` will call `panic!` if the buffer is not long enough. Finally, `has_samples` simply returns whether or not there are any more samples in the stream.

Using this API directly might look like this:

```
let mut stream: AudioStream = ...;
let mut buffer = vec![0.0; stream.num_channels()];

while stream.has_samples() {
    stream.read_samples(&mut buffer);
    play_samples(&buffer);
}
```

Not the worst, but there are some obvious flaws. A major one is that buffer allocation is the user's responsibility, opening up the potential for bugs. Also, the caller ensures that there are actually samples to read before trying to read the samples from the stream. Ideally, we want to put an abstraction around this pattern so that the user only has to worry about what to do with the decoded samples.

Since `AudioStream` produces a sequence of values, the `Iterator` abstraction seems like the obvious pattern to use, so let us do that:

```
impl Iterator for AudioStream {
    type Item = Vec<f32>;

    fn next(&mut self) -> Option<Vec<f32>> {
        // Make sure there are samples
```

```
        if !self.has_samples() {
            return None;
        }
        // Create the buffer
        let num_channels = self.num_channels();
        let mut buffer = vec![0.0; num_channels];

        // Read and return the samples
        self.read_samples(&mut buffer);
        Some(buffer)
    }
}
```

This will work fine in a for loop and abstracts away the details so that the user cannot misuse the API. Under careful observation, though, you might notice that it is not identical to the previous example. With the iterator, we are allocating a new `Vec<f32>` on each iteration. This is extra overhead compared to the original loop where we simply re-used the same buffer over and over.

What would it look like if we tried to make an iterator that re-used a buffer?

```
struct Iter<'a> {
  stream: &'a mut AudioStream,
  buffer: Vec<f32>
}

impl<'a> Iter<'a> {
  fn new(stream: &'a mut AudioStream) -> Iter<'a> {
    let num_channels = stream.num_channels();
    Iter {
      stream: stream,
      buffer: vec![0.0; num_channels]
    }
  }
}

impl<'a> Iterator for Iter<'a> {
  type Item = &[f32]; // error: missing lifetime

  fn next(&mut self) -> Option<&[f32]> {
    if !self.stream.has_samples() {
      None
    } else {
```

```
      self.stream.read_samples(&mut self.buffer);
      // error: conflicting lifetime requirements
      Some(&self.buffer)
    }
  }
}
```

Trying to compile the previous example will give you a number of errors, and while you can "fix" some of them, it is impossible to fix all of them. Eventually, you will run into a situation where removing one error will cause another and the fix for that error results in the previous error. The issue here is that the lifetime of any reference given out by the iterator must live as long as the iterator itself. However, the standard iterator trait gives us no way to express this.

This is where the Streaming Iterator pattern comes in. This pattern adopts the same idea as `Iterator`, combining producing the next value with indicating that there are no more values, but in a more ad-hoc manner.

A streaming iterator version of the previous would look like this:

```
struct StreamIter<'a> {
  stream: &'a mut AudioStream,
  buffer: Vec<f32>
}

impl<'a> StreamIter<'a> {
  fn next<'b>(&'b mut self) -> Option<&'b [f32]> {
    if !self.stream.has_samples() {
      None
    } else {
      self.stream.read_samples(&mut self.buffer);
      Some(&self.buffer)
    }
  }
}
```

It is almost identical to the previous example (the `new` method has been excluded for brevity). However, this example actually compiles. There are two significant differences compared to the iterator we tried to build.

Firstly, we do not use a trait. This is not only because there is no standard `StreamingIterator` trait, but also because Rust lacks the ability to construct a generally useful `StreamingIterator` trait. It is not the case, however, that

Rust cannot provide a `StreamingIterator` trait. The issue is that Rust cannot generally provide iterator adapters that work on a `StreamingIterator` due to the lifetime restrictions necessary to prevent re-allocating the buffer.

Secondly, the `next` method has a lifetime parameter linking together `self` and the return value. This means that you cannot call the `next` method while the previously returned value is still present. Looking at how the method is implemented, this makes sense. If you could call `next` while the previous set of samples was around, the method would overwrite those samples.

Using this streaming iterator looks like this:

```
let mut stream = StreamIter::new(audio_stream);

while let Some(samples) = stream.next() {
    play_samples(samples);
}
```

This uses the `while let` to combine the loop and match we would otherwise need. Using `while let` makes streaming iterators almost as easy to work with as regular iterators.

## LIMITATIONS

Streaming iterators is a useful pattern, but not without their flaws. As mentioned earlier, trying to create a `StreamingIterator` trait is difficult at best and impossible due to the lifetime restrictions necessary. This means that all those iterator adapters provided for regular iterators are unavailable for your streaming iterator.

So, when should you use one? There are two requirements for using streaming iterators:

1. The restriction with which you cannot get the next value while the current one is around is unimportant. There are two reasons why this might be the case: 1) there is no expected reason for a user to want or need multiple values from the stream, or 2) you expect users to almost always transform the produced values.

2. You can take advantage of the previous requirement to improve performance. This is important as there is no reason to reach for streaming iterators when there is no performance gain from it.

Both requirements should be met before you reach for streaming iterators. The example used meets both the requirements well:

1. Audio samples are independent of each other. While some use cases might want multiple samples, those cases would likely transform the samples in some way, anyway.
2. Audio playback is timing sensitive, so, increased performance is always desirable. We were able to reuse the buffer for samples across iterations instead of allocating and de-allocating a new one every time.

The Iterator and Streaming Iterator concepts are very useful, but they do not allow you to modify the collection that you are sequencing over. Luckily, there is a related abstraction known as Cursors that provides that functionality.

## CURSORS

Cursors are a pattern for traversing and modifying collections. Iterators and streaming iterators are independent of collections since iteration is a general concept that is not specific to a collection; remember, we can provide iterators over random numbers being generated. Where iterators only provide the ability to iterate over a collection, cursors are much more general. Cursors provide a way of iterating over and *modifying* an underlying collection. While we can reuse the `Iterator` trait to iterate over the collection, there are many ways to modify a collection and they tend to be fairly specific to an individual collection. For example, you can insert at a specific index in a `Vec`, but you have no control over where you insert with a `HashSet`. So, we cannot provide a generic trait that allows the cursor concept to be generically reusable, as with the `Iterator` trait, because different collections have different means of modification. Instead, we can implement specific methods of modification that are useful for each underlying collection. In this way, cursors are more tightly linked to their underlying collection.

There are two pieces of functionality that cursors possess – movement and modification. Movement refers to the ability to move the cursor around inside the collection, either a specific location or relative to the current location. Modification refers to the ability to modify the collection at the cursor's location. This can be insertion, deletion or replacement.

Cursors are commonly found when working with files. The location where a program is currently reading or writing is a cursor. There are functions for moving the cursor to the start or end of the file, as well as a number of bytes forwards or backwards. Writing to a file is a modification at the cursor location.

To demonstrate cursors, we will build one for a list. Figure 6-4 shows that the cursor's position is considered to be before the element of the same index.

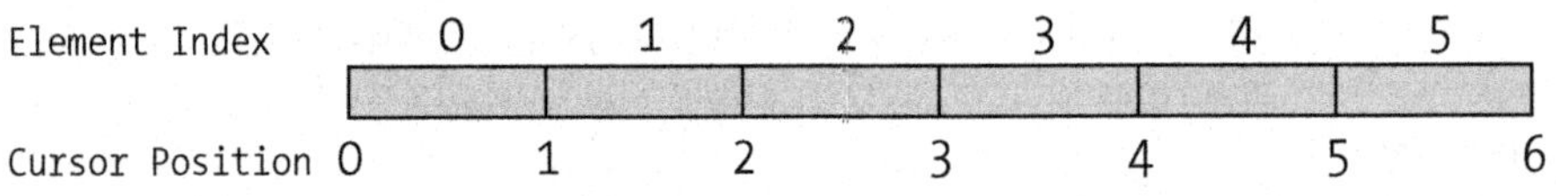


**Figure 6-4:** Cursor position relative to element index

Figure 6-5 shows that the cursor movement will be relative, moving forwards and backwards, one element at a time. If the cursor is at either end of the list, it can only move away from the end of the list.

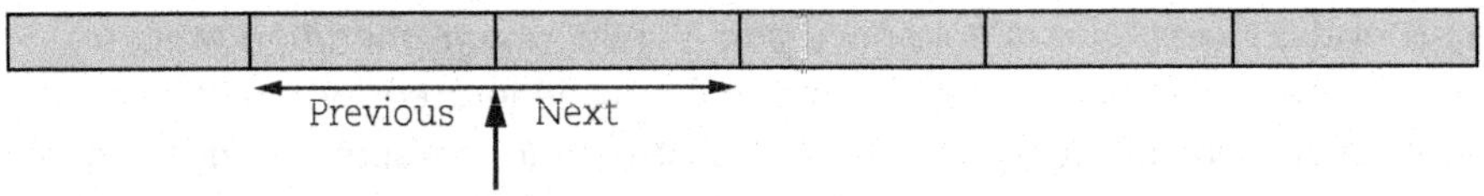


**Figure 6-5:** Cursor movement

We will support two modification operations – insertion and deletion. Figure 6-6 shows how insertion will insert an element after the cursor's position and leave the cursor in the same position.

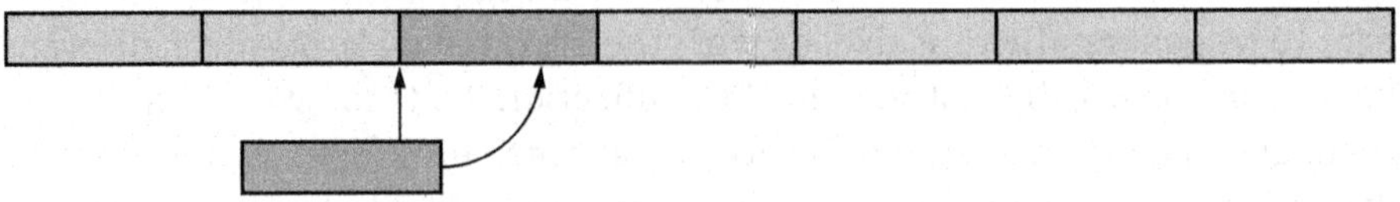

**Figure 6-6:** Inserting a new element

Deletion will remove the element after the cursor's position, again leaving the cursor's position unchanged, as seen in Figure 6-7.

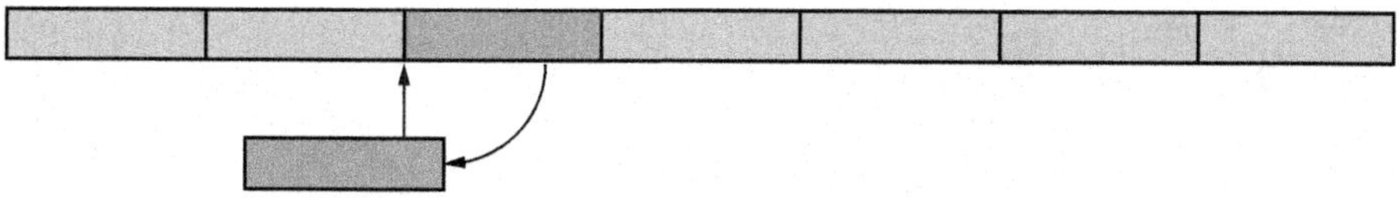

**Figure 6-7:** Removing an element

We will use the standard library's `Vec` as our list and track the position using an index. Our cursor, therefore, looks like this:

```
pub struct Cursor<'a, T: 'a> {
  vec: &'a mut Vec<T>,
  idx: usize
}

impl<'a, T> Cursor<'a, T> {
  pub fn new(vec: &'a mut Vec<T>) -> Cursor<'a,T> {
    Cursor {
      vec: vec,
      idx: 0
    }
  }
}
```

A `new` method has been included for constructing the cursor from a vector.

Next, we will implement the movement functionality. As with iterators, we will combine movement with getting a value.

```
impl<'a, T> Cursor<'a, T> {
  pub fn next<'b>(&'b mut self)
                 -> Option<&'b mut T> {
    let idx = self.idx;
    if idx < self.vec.len() {
      self.idx += 1;
    }
    self.vec.get_mut(idx)
  }

  pub fn prev<'b>(&'b mut self)
                 -> Option<&'b mut T> {
```

```
      if self.idx > 0 {
        self.idx -= 1;
        self.vec.get_mut(self.idx)
      } else {
        None
      }
    }
  }
```

Both methods adjust the index and then return a reference to the element they just moved over. If the cursor is at either end of the vector, then the index is not changed and None is returned instead.

The second part of the cursor functionality is modification:

```
impl<'a, T> Cursor<'a, T> {
  pub fn insert(&mut self, val: T) {
    self.vec.insert(self.idx, val);
  }

  pub fn remove(&mut self) -> Option<T> {
    if self.idx >= self.vec.len() {
      None
    } else {
      Some(self.vec.remove(self.idx))
    }
  }
}
```

These modification functions represent the power of cursors. Iterators do not allow modification of the collection being iterated over, as that modification may cause references to become invalid. The cursor, on the other hand, merely tracks an index into the vector. By using an index, insertion and deletion of elements does not invalidate any references.

Cursors are most useful for data structures where modification may not result in references being invalidated. Doubly linked lists are a good example, as each node is independent of the others and insertion of a new node will not cause any references to be invalidated. Other data structures have similar properties that can be exploited, especially when unsafe code is used.

Cursors are a useful pattern for the implementation of data structures. Data structures often need to rely on unsafe code for performance or to work around language limitations. Cursors are able to provide safe access to functionality that would otherwise be difficult or impossible to expose safely.

## KEY TAKEAWAYS

- Iterators provide a way to operate on a sequence of data.
- The Rust standard library provides many methods on iterators that produce Iterator Adapters – iterators in their own rights that modify the iterator they are adapting in specific ways.
- Implementing your own iterator can be very simple if you are creating a custom data structure. Doing so automatically gives the users of your iterator access to all of the iterator adapters defined by the standard library.
- The Streaming Iterator pattern is not, and will not, be defined by the standard library, but can be useful to implement yourself if you want to provide a way to reuse a common buffer in an iterator-like manner.
- Cursors are similar to iterators but they also provide the ability to modify the underlying container that they operate on.

# 7

# Concurrency

Often, when writing software, we want to have the ability to do more than one thing at a time, or concurrently. If we are writing highly user-interactive software – such as a graphical user interface – we want our program to always be responsive to the user, even when we need to perform very long-running operations. What do we mean by a long-running operation? One instance of a long-running operation could be data processing on a large data set. Perhaps you need to analyze a large audio file that might take several seconds or even minutes to process. Another instance of a long-running operation occurs not when your program is doing anything but, rather, your program is waiting on the operating system to perform some action on its behalf. Maybe your program needs to communicate over a network or is reading or writing large files from a disk. Either of these actions can take several seconds or minutes to complete. Pausing a user interface for even several seconds is unacceptable if you are trying to create responsive, highly-interactive software. Ideally, we want to be able to service our user interface at the same time as we are performing our long-running operations. We want to be able to do both operations concurrently.

Another example of concurrency occurs, not when we want to perform different long-running operations at the same time, but when we want to concurrently perform multiple instances of the same algorithm on different data sets to take advantage of multiple CPU cores that are commonly found in microprocessors today. One of the classic examples of this is a network service. For every network connection that comes in, we want to run the same algorithm – the network server. The more instances of the network server that we have running, the better we are able to take advantage of the multiple processor cores that microprocessors provide.

The main operating system abstraction for implementing concurrency in a program is called threads. A thread (or thread of execution) is a sequence of instructions that is scheduled for execution by the operating system. Every program has at least one thread associated with it – the main thread. The operating system provides facilities to create additional threads of execution that run concurrently with the main thread. In the case of a single CPU core, the operating system emulates concurrent execution by time-slicing the processor and switching between the executing threads many times in a second. In the case of multiple CPU cores, the operating system can schedule threads to truly run at the same time by executing different threads on the different CPU cores. Even then, the operating system will time-slice the cores so that more threads than CPU cores can exist in the system.

The threads of a program natively exist in the same address space for the process that they run in. This means that, from an operating system perspective, each thread has access to all of the memory that the process has access to. This leads to data races when multiple threads are trying to modify the same location of memory, since the independent threads can stomp on each other. To aid the programmer in preventing data races, the operating system provides locking constructs to help ensure that only one thread is executing in the critical section at a time and modifying shared memory locations.

Rust has type-system level support for threading and for protecting the threaded program from data races. In low-level systems languages like C, the programming language has no concept of threads — they are provided solely by libraries provided by the operating system. Thus, the compiler cannot provide any assistance to ensure that your concurrent program does not contain races. Some languages, like Java, allow you to opt-in to language-based concurrency protection. However, with the support being opt-in, it is easy for a programmer to overlook adding protections where necessary. Since Rust encodes threading support into the type system, the Rust compiler can enforce that data is accessed in a thread-safe manner. In this chapter, we will look at two different mechanisms that Rust provides to enable the programmer to efficiently and safely write concurrent programs. These two mechanisms are: native support for efficient message passing and native support for safely using shared memory. First, we will look in depth at message passing.

## MESSAGE PASSING CONCURRENCY

Rust has native support for threading and for passing messages between threads. Conceptually, message passing is one of the simplest forms of communicating between threads because all of the data is shared explicitly by the programmer through the exchange of messages that are passed back and forth between threads.

To see how message passing works in Rust, let us imagine a simple example. We have some program that needs to read a large file; at the same time, we need to be able to display to the user some sort of status to let them know that the program is still working. For an interactive command line program, it is common to periodically print a dot to the screen to let the user know that the program has not hung, so we will print a dot to the screen every second that the program is reading the file, until the whole file has been read.

To implement our status output, we will push our file-read operation to a background thread and use the main thread of the program to display the status to the user. When the file is completely read, we will print out the contents of the file. Figure 7-1 shows the sequence of steps that our program takes to read the file in the background and still perform work in the foreground.

**Figure 7-1:** Background read of a file using message passing

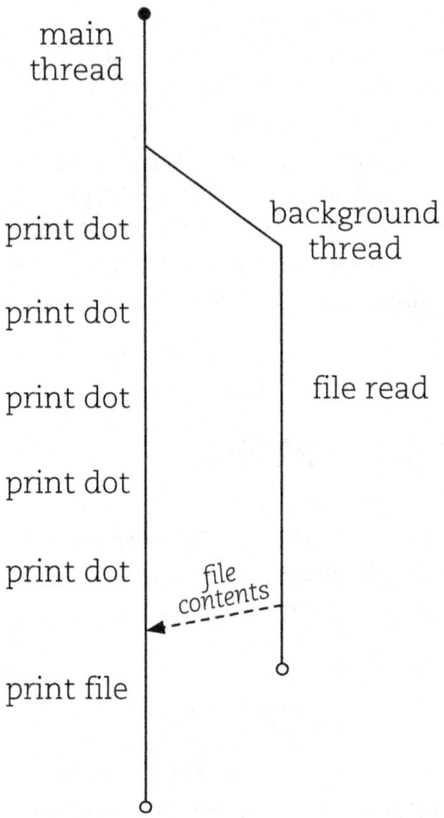


In Figure 7-1, each of the solid lines represents the execution of a thread. Early in the run-time of the main thread, a background thread is spawned and begins its own execution. The open circles at the end of the solid lines represent the ending of a thread of execution. Once the background thread starts up, the background thread begins reading the file. When the file-read operation is complete, the file contents are sent back to the main thread through some message-passing interface, represented by the dashed line in the diagram. Shortly after sending the message, the background thread can end. Concurrent with the execution of the backgrounded file-read operation, the main thread needs to check to see if the file is complete and, if it is not, print a dot to the screen. When the main thread receives the file, it prints the file contents out to the console.

To handle sending the complete file between threads, we are going to use Rust's `channel` mechanism. A `channel` in Rust is a unidirectional message-passing interface between two or more threads. More specifically, a channel consists of a Receiver<T> endpoint that can be accessed by a single thread and a Sender<T> endpoint that can be used by one or more threads to send messages to the receiving endpoint. A message can be any type that implements the Send trait.

### The Send and Sync Traits

The Send trait is used by Rust to indicate that the implementing type can safely have its ownership transferred between threads. The Send trait is automatically implemented by the compiler if all portions of the data type implement Send. All of the primitive types implement Send, as do most of the standard library types. One notable example of a type that does not implement Send is the Rc type – the ref-counted pointer type – since the manipulation of the reference count is not handled in a thread-safe manner so that single-threaded use of the Rc type is as efficient as possible. Instead, the standard library provides an Arc type that does implement Send to enable you to have a thread-safe ref-counted pointer.

The Sync trait is used by Rust to indicate that a reference (&T) to the type implements the Send trait. Types that support interior mutability like a Cell or a RefCell do not implement Sync. If you need to get the interior mutability back, you can wrap the type in some sort of locking construct like a Mutex or a RWLock (to be discussed later in the chapter).

Often, we will define an enum that lets us send different messages along the same channel, but we can send other types, such as a String, through as well. We can see how that works in practice using our example program:

```
use std::sync::mpsc;
use std::thread;

fn do_foreground_work() {...}

fn do_background_read() -> mpsc::Receiver<String> {
    let (send, recv) = mpsc::channel();
    let _ = thread::spawn(move || {
        let data = do_large_read();
        send.send(data).unwrap();
    });

    recv
}
```

```
fn main() {
    let recv = do_background_read();

    loop {
        match recv.try_recv() {
            Ok(data) => {
                println!("{:?}", data);
                break;
            }
            Err(mpsc::TryRecvError::Disconnected) => {
                println!("disconnected without data");
                break;
            }
            Err(mpsc::TryRecvError::Empty) => {
                do_foreground_work();
            }
        };
    }
}
```

In our example program, we define a function called do_background_read() that creates a channel, spawns a thread to do our large read, and moves the send side of the channel into the thread. We can move the send side of the channel, a Sender<String>, into the thread since the Sender<T> type implements Send.

Once the background thread starts up, the large file is read and the result is sent out on the channel when the read is complete. It is interesting to note that the send method on the Sender<T> can fail if the receive side of the channel has already been dropped before the send occurs. If the send succeeds, the message is accepted by the channel. Note, however, that the successful send does not mean that the message has been delivered since the send method is asynchronous for Sender<T>.

The return type of our do_background_read function is the Receiver<String> type. This allows the function to return the receive side of the channel to the caller so that the main thread can get the result of the background read when it is complete. From our main thread, we loop waiting on the receive side of the channel to have data available. With each loop, we attempt to receive data from the channel using the try_recv method. If a message is available, the message is returned in the Result. Otherwise, we can get one of two errors:

- either the other side of the channel has disconnected (which should not happen in this example) or
- the channel did not have data available yet (it was empty).

If the channel was empty, our main thread can go ahead and do the foreground work that we set aside for our main thread to perform. If we actually got data, though, then we consume that data by printing it out.

Since we needed to perform some processing in the foreground while the background read was processing, we performed what is known as a non-blocking receive (or a "try receive") on the channel. Instead of blocking the main thread and waiting for data to be available, we polled the channel to see if there was data to process. If we did not have foreground work to do, but still needed to push that large read to a background thread, we could have performed a blocking read of the channel like the following:

```
fn main() {
    let recv1 = do_background_read();
    let recv2 = do_background_read();
    println!("{:?}", recv1.recv().unwrap());
    println!("{:?}", recv2.recv().unwrap());
}
```

In the above code snippet, we are concurrently executing two background reads, in two separate threads. However, we do not have any foreground work to do, so we can just block the main thread until the first background read is completed. Then, if the second background read is not complete, the main thread will block again until it is done. Since the recv method blocks until data is available, it will either return valid data or an error stating that the other side has disconnected.

## An Active Queue Mechanism

If your program makes a lot of use of short-lived threads to kick computations out of the main thread and into the background, you may notice that the creation time of a short-lived thread can dominate the run-time of the task that you are trying to execute. Thread creation is ultimately delegated to the operating system, which involves a context switch into the kernel to kick off the new thread. This could take hundreds of microseconds to accomplish where the operating system is performing work that is not the work that you want your program to do. It would be useful to have a thread waiting around in the background, ready to do work for us, that we could just submit work to. Since a `channel` can be used to send arbitrary types between threads, could we use a `channel` to send closures to a background thread so that we can avoid creating a lot of short-lived background threads? Yes, we can with the `ActiveQueue` abstraction, as seen in Figure 7-2.

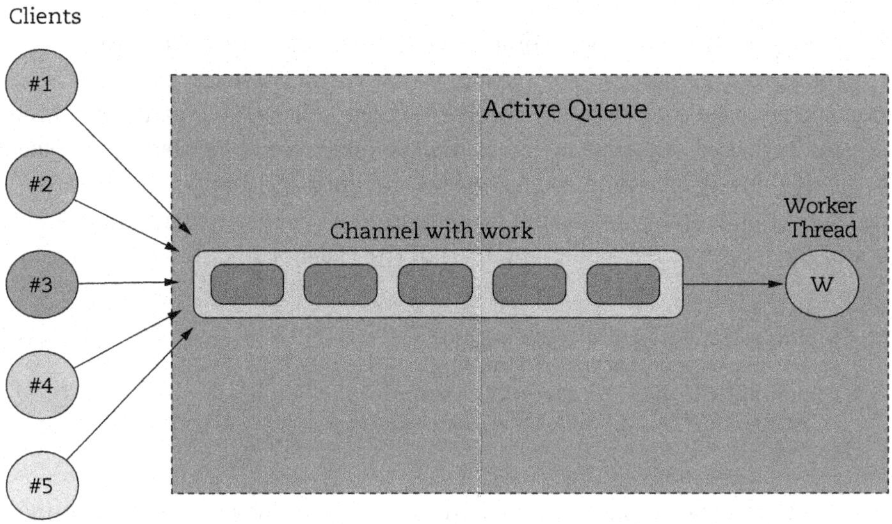


**Figure 7-2:** An ActiveQueue accepting work from multiple clients

In Figure 7-2, we see that an `ActiveQueue` consists of a channel that contains some sort of work (that we will represent using closures) and a worker thread. This worker thread receives work to execute from the receive side of a channel. The send side of the channel can be used to submit work to the `ActiveQueue` and can be cloned and moved into other threads. This allows independent threads to execute particular work synchronously, since the `ActiveQueue` will only process a single work item at a time from the channel. The following code snippet shows an example implementation of an `ActiveQueue`:

```
use std::sync::mpsc;
use std::thread;
pub type Work = Box<FnMut() + Send>;

pub struct ActiveQueue {
    send: mpsc::SyncSender<Work>,
    join: thread::JoinHandle<()>,
```

```
}

impl ActiveQueue {
    pub fn new(bound: usize) -> ActiveQueue {
        let (snd, rcv) = mpsc::sync_channel(bound);

        let join = thread::spawn(move || {
            loop {
                let mut work: Work = rcv.recv().unwrap();
                work();
            }
        });
        ActiveQueue {
            send: snd,
            join: join,
        }
    }
    pub fn send<T>(&self, work: T)
      where T: FnMut() + Send + 'static
    {
        self.send.send(Box::new(work)).unwrap();
    }
        pub fn wait(self) {
        self.join.join().unwrap();
    }
}
```

In our `ActiveQueue` abstraction, we are declaring our message type to be `Work = Box<FnMut() + Send>`, which just means that it can be a closure that mutably captures variables and whose environment consists of variables that implement the `Send` trait. The variables in the environment of the closure must all implement `Send` since the environment will be sent to the `ActiveQueue` worker thread for execution.

Our `ActiveQueue` consists of a single background thread that receives the `Work` messages from a `sync_channel` instead of a `channel`. The `ActiveQueue` struct contains the send side of the `sync_channel` and a `JoinHandle<()>` that represents the background thread. The `sync_channel` creates a bounded `channel`, which means it can only hold a finite number of messages that have not been processed by the receiver without blocking the sender. In our `ActiveQueue` example, we represent that finite number of messages as the `bound` parameter passed into the `new` method on the `ActiveQueue`. The `JoinHandle<()>` that is returned by the `thread::spawn` can be used to wait on the thread to complete. The type parameter passed for the `JoinHandle<_>`

matches the return type of the thread closure itself. It can be used to retrieve a value from the thread when it completes (although that functionality is not used in this example). Since this thread closure does not return any value, we use a () as the type parameter.

When the background thread receives Work over the channel, it then executes the Work in that background thread. This allows us to only take the hit of thread creation once for these short-lived tasks that need to execute in the background, as long as the short-lived tasks do not need to execute concurrently with each other.

Using the ActiveQueue is fairly straightforward. We create an instance of the ActiveQueue and, to execute tasks on the background thread, we send the closures to the ActiveQueue instead of spawning new threads to execute them. Finally, we pause our main thread until the background thread completes (which it never will in this example) so that the main thread does not prematurely cause the program to exit.

```
fn main() {
    let queue = ActiveQueue::new(10);
    queue.send(|| {
        println!("Hello, world!");
    });
    queue.send(|| {
        println!("Hello, world again!");
    });
    queue.wait();
}
```

So, using our channel (and sync_channel) abstraction, we can have some amount of communication between our main thread and background threads. We can send data values between the threads and even send complete tasks between the threads. However, when we send the data between threads, we are transferring ownership. When the transfer between threads is complete, the sending thread no longer has access to the data due to Rust's ownership rules. We need to have some way to truly share data between threads that can be modified by the sharing threads in such a way that it does not cause a concurrency problem.

# SHARED MEMORY CONCURRENCY

Let us now look at the idea of sharing memory from a Rust point-of-view. When we create a thread, we can send data to the thread by ownership. If we try to go down the path of sending data by reference to the threads, we rapidly run into lifetime issues unless the data that we are passing has a static lifetime, as seen in the following snippet:

```
let data = vec![1, 2, 3, 4];
for _ in 0..5 {
    let data = &data;
    thread::spawn(move || {
        println!("data = {:?}", data);
    });
}

error: 'data' does not live long enough
   --> src/main.rs:97:21
    |
97  |         let data = &data;
    |                     ^^^^ does not live long enough
...
102 | }
    | - borrowed value only lives until here
    |
    = note: borrowed value must be valid for the static lifetime...
error: aborting due to previous error
```

If we think about how the compiler allocates memory for data, this makes perfect sense. When you create a variable, data is allocated for that variable on the stack. If you share a reference to that data with another thread, the other thread has its own stack and the compiler cannot guarantee that the thread that originally shared the data will live long enough since the thread that owns the data could end – freeing its stack when it does. If the owning thread ends before the thread with the reference ends, the referencing thread will have a dangling reference to the data. We can see an idea of what might happen in Figure 7-3.

Figure 7-3: Thought experiment of sharing references between threads

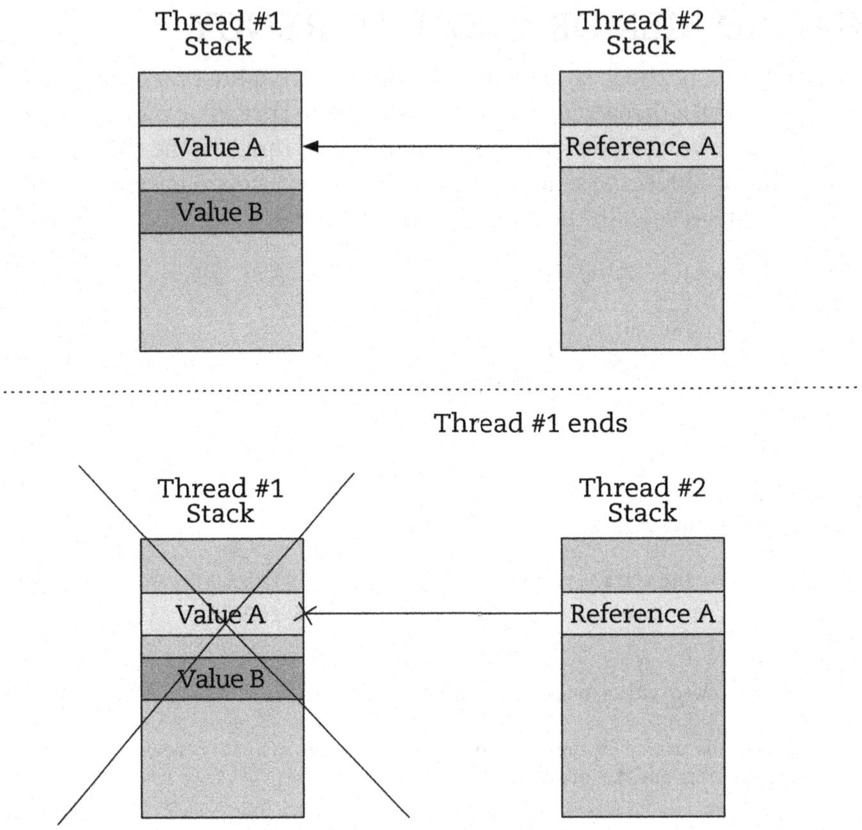


To prevent a possible dangling reference on Thread #2 when Thread #1 ends, the Rust compiler only allows you to share references to static data between threads. Alternatively, you can bypass the problem completely by passing allocating data on the heap and then using a ref-counted pointer to share references to data between threads.

The Rust standard library provides a data type that is meant for sharing references to data between threads – the `Arc` data type. The `Arc` data type is an Atomic, Reference-Counted pointer to data allocated from the heap. By using an `Arc`, you can easily share immutable data between threads. In the following example, we are wrapping our vector up in an `Arc`, so that the vector is allocated on the heap and we have a ref-counted pointer to the data. Then, when we `clone` the `data` variable, we have two references to the vector, one of which is moved into the new thread where we can access it.

```
use std::sync::Arc;
use std::thread::sleep;
use std::time::Duration;
let data = Arc::new(vec![1, 2, 3, 4]);
for _ in 0..5 {
    let data = data.clone();
    thread::spawn(move || {
        println!("data = {:?}", data);
    });
}
sleep(Duration::new(1, 0));
```

Although the data variable is an Arc, we can just print out the data because the Arc provides an implementation of the Deref trait into a &T, in this case into a &Vec<usize>. However, Arc does not provide an implementation of DerefMut, so we cannot coerce the Arc into a &mut Vec<usize>. The Rust language goes to great pains to prevent multiple mutable references to a single piece of data. If the standard library allowed the Arc to coerce to a &mut T, then there is a chance that two concurrently running threads will both have mutable references to the same piece of data, violating one of the core safety tenets of Rust.

To protect data from being modified by two threads at the same time, we need to lock the data before we modify it. When the data is locked, other threads cannot read or write the data. Rust provides a Mutex abstraction to allow you to lock the data before you can access it.

```
use std::sync::Mutex;
use std::sync::Arc;

let data = Arc::new(Mutex::new(vec![]));
for x in 0..5 {
    let data = data.clone();
    thread::spawn(move || {
        let mut data = data.lock().unwrap();
        data.push(x);
        println!("data = {:?}", *data);
    });
}
```

A mutex is an operating system construct that provide MUTually-EXclusive access to a data structure. That is, a mutex provides the programmer with the ability to control access to a data structure and enforce that only a single thread of execution can access it at a time. Using the raw, primitive mutex operations, the programmer is responsible for correctly locking and unlocking the mutex before every access to the data structure. If the programmer forgets to lock the data structure before use, nothing in the system prevents access to the data structure – it is just used in an unprotected manner. Fortunately, Rust provides a `Mutex` abstraction that is more robust than the raw, primitive operations.

The Rust `Mutex` abstraction completely controls access to the underlying data structure since the `Mutex` owns the data that it protects. When the lock method is called on the `Mutex`, the `Mutex` calls the underlying lock primitive that protects access to the data and returns a `MutexGuard<T>` that implements `Deref<T>` and `DerefMut<T>` which provide a way to borrow the underlying data structure. When the `MutexGuard<T>` goes out of scope, it unlocks the underlying `Mutex`. This provides a much stronger guarantee than the primitive mutex operations. The programmer can no longer forget to lock the mutex before accessing the data and to unlock the mutex when they are finished with it.

By wrapping our `Vec` inside of a `Mutex` before we store it in the `Arc`, we are required to lock the vector in the thread before we go to read or write from the vector. Locking the data structure prevents any other threads in the system from being able to read or write the data structure while the current thread has it locked. This preserves Rust's requirement that there can only be one mutable reference to a piece of data at a time.

However, using a `Mutex` in this manner is a little overly cautious. The `Mutex` allows only a single reference, mutable or immutable, to a piece of data at a time, while Rust generally allows as many simultaneous, immutable, references to data as we would like. To work around this, Rust has a `RwLock`, or a reader-writer lock. With a `RwLock`, you specify how you want to acquire the lock – for read or for write. A `RwLock` allows you to have multiple threads concurrently acquire the lock for reading as long as no thread holds the lock for writing; however, you can only have one thread acquire the lock for writing when zero threads are holding the lock for reading. This added flexibility does come with a slight run-time cost since the `RwLock` has to do book-keeping to keep track of the number of readers currently holding the lock. Generally speaking, though, if you have the need to have many readers at the same time, taking the slight run-time hit for the lock is more than covered by the decrease in lock contention. We can rewrite our example using the RwLock and gain a bit more fine-grained access to our data.

```
use std::sync::RwLock;
use std::sync::Arc;

let data = Arc::new(RwLock::new(vec![]));
for x in 0..5 {
    let data = data.clone();
    thread::spawn(move || {
        {
            let mut data = data.write().unwrap();
            data.push(x);
        }
        let data = data.read().unwrap();
        println!("data = {:?}", *data);
    });
}
```

In this example, when we go to insert into our vector, we acquire the lock using the `write` method to specify that we are going to modify the vector. No other thread can hold the lock during this time. Once we release the lock – when the guard goes out of scope – we then acquire the lock using the `read` method to specify that we just want to immutably access the data. Any number of threads can hold the lock for reading, so multiple threads can be printing the vector at the same time.

After our exploration of shared memory concurrency, we are ready to take a look at a refinement to the `ActiveQueue` concept, the `ThreadPool`.

## A ThreadPool Mechanism

The `ActiveQueue` abstraction that we previously created used a `channel` and a background thread to create a data structure that sequentially executed closures in a background thread without having to endure the startup time of a thread for every closure we wanted to run in the background. The `ActiveQueue` works quite nicely if you want the closures run on it to be run sequentially with respect to one another. However, the `ActiveQueue` will only use a single thread, so it may not be efficiently taking into account the processor resources you have available. If the work you need to run in the background can be run concurrently with each other and you want to be able to fully use your processor resources, a `ThreadPool` may be more effective. With a ThreadPool, you specify the number of background threads you want to create and, when you submit work to the ThreadPool, the next available background thread will start executing the work.

In Figure 7-4, we can see the general design for a ThreadPool. In it, we need to have some sort of thread-safe queue for storing outstanding work, some number of worker threads, and a way to wake up the worker threads when new work is added to the queue.

**Figure 7-4:** Thread pool with multiple background threads

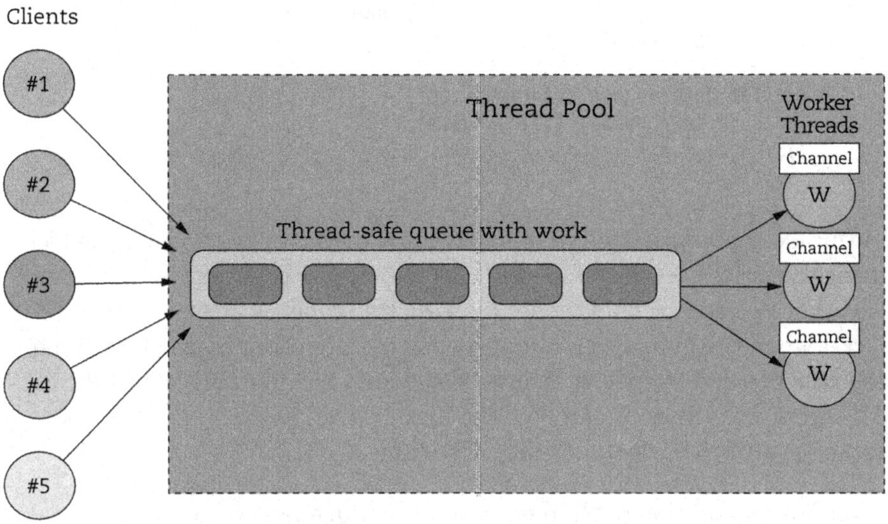


Let us take a look at our ThreadPool implementation, starting with our type definitions:

```
use std::collections::VecDeque;
use std::sync::{Arc, mpsc, Mutex};
use std::thread;

pub type Work = Box<FnMut() + Send>;
type Queue = Arc<Mutex<VecDeque<Work>>>;

enum Message { CheckForWork, Quit }

struct PoolHandle {
    send: mpsc::Sender<Message>,
    join: thread::JoinHandle<()>,
}
```

```
pub struct ThreadPool {
    queue: Queue,
    threads: Vec<PoolHandle>,
}
```

Our ThreadPool consists of two parts:

- a Queue that is a Mutex-locked data structure containing our Work and
- a vector of our thread handles which are contained in a Vec<PoolHandle>.

The PoolHandle consists of a JoinHandle, which allows us to wait for the thread to complete, and the sending-side of a channel for a Message type. The Message type is used to instruct the background thread whether it needs to wake up and check for more work or to quit executing.

Why do we have a Queue for Work instead of just using a channel like we did with the ActiveQueue? In the ActiveQueue case, we can use a channel since there is only one background thread to receive messages. Remember, a channel can have multiple senders, but only a single receiver. By storing our Work on a Queue, we can use the channel to wake up all of the threads independently and, whichever thread is idle and wakes up first, can fetch Work from the Queue. With that in mind, let us look at the logic needed to create our background thread:

```
fn create(queue: Queue, recv: mpsc::Receiver<Message>) ->
thread::JoinHandle<()> {
    thread::spawn(move || {
        loop {
            match recv.recv().unwrap() {
                Message::Quit => {
                    break;
                }
                Message::CheckForWork => {
                    let work = {
                        let mut queue = queue.lock().unwrap();
                        queue.pop_front()
                    };
                    if let Some(mut thunk) = work {
                        thunk();
                    }
                }
            }
        }
    })
}
```

Our thread creation function takes in our Queue and the Receiver<Message> that will let us control the thread. We spawn the thread into the background and loop around, receiving messages from the channel. When we receive a Quit message, we break out of our loop, which will implicitly end the thread. When we receive the CheckForWork message, we lock the Queue and attempt to pop Work out of the Queue. If we received Work, we then execute the closure.

Now that we know how our background threads will work, creating our ThreadPool is easy and is a straightforward extension of our ThreadPool type and the create function:

```
impl ThreadPool {
    pub fn new(num_threads: usize) -> ThreadPool {
        let queue: Queue = Arc::new(Mutex::new(VecDeque::new()));
        let mut threads = Vec::with_capacity(num_threads);
        for _ in 0..num_threads {
            let (send, recv) = mpsc::channel();
            let join = create(queue.clone(), recv);
            threads.push(PoolHandle {
                send: send,
                join: join,
            });
        }

        ThreadPool {
            queue: queue,
            threads: threads,
        }
    }
    pub fn add_work<T>(&mut self, work: T)
        where T: FnMut() + Send + 'static
    {
        {
            let mut queue = self.queue.lock().unwrap();
            queue.push_back(Box::new(work));
        }

        for thread in &self.threads {
           thread.send.send(Message::CheckForWork).unwrap();
        }
    }
}
```

The add_work function is defined similarly to the add_work function for the ActiveQueue. Instead of sending the Work across the channel, though, we add it to the back of the `Queue` and then notify each thread using the dedicated per-thread `channel` that it needs to check for work. This is a critical design idea of the `ThreadPool` – we add one piece of work to the queue, yet we notify every thread. Whichever thread is not currently executing work and wakes up first will be able to retrieve work from the queue. The other threads will not receive work from the queue and will block waiting for the wake-up message again. However, when multiple pieces of work are added to our `ThreadPool`, they will run concurrently up to the number of threads we have running in our `ThreadPool`.

## KEY TAKEAWAYS

- Rust uses the static type system to restrict how data is shared between threads. The simplest manner of sharing data is to wrap up the changes in a message whose ownership is transferred between threads.
- Rust also allows shared memory concurrency. It uses the type system to enforce that mutable data must be locked before it is accessed from multiple threads.
- Rust makes it easy to send work between threads by wrapping the work up in a closure. For short-lived work tasks, it is typically more efficient to send work to a pre-existing background thread like an `ActiveQueue` or a `ThreadPool`.

# 8

# Type-Safe Idiomatic Code

Several programming idioms and design patterns crop up when writing Rust code. But first, what is a programming idiom? Typically, what we mean by a programming idiom is a way of writing code that is not enforced by the programming language but rather a way of expressing common recurring design concepts in programs. A design pattern is simply a named expression of a particular idiom that gives developers a common vocabulary when talking about programming idioms.

How are design patterns different from traits, then? A trait gives a programmer a way of expressing a concept so that generic code can be written to work with the design. A design pattern goes beyond that. With design patterns, the general idea behind the code might be common among multiple implementations, but the specific interface is different, so a trait cannot apply. As we will see, this is the case with the Builder pattern. Alternatively, a trait might apply to a portion of the pattern, but cannot be used to fully specify the semantics of how the pattern works, which is the case with the `Drop` trait and the RAII pattern. Lastly, a design pattern might be describing an interrelated group of types that have no common interface but all work together as we will see in our type-safe state machines.

Each of the patterns we will describe in this chapter are commonly found when working with Rust code, either in the standard library or in third-party crates. Each pattern is meant to help ensure that the Rust static type system is giving the programmer as much assistance as possible to prevent the programmer from making errors. First, we will look at the Builder pattern.

## THE BUILDER PATTERN

One of the tenets of memory safety is that you can never have a dangling reference — the Rust compiler goes to great lengths to prevent you from having a reference to an object that no longer exists. But, what prevents you from have a reference to an object that is only partially created? What do we even mean by a partially created object, anyway? Let us look at a quick example:

```
struct Person {
  name: String,
  address: Option<Address>,
}

impl Person {
  pub fn new(name: &str) -> Person {
    Person { name: name.into(), address: None }
  }
  pub fn set_address(&mut self, addr: Address) {
    self.address = Some(addr);
  }
  pub fn mail_package(&self) -> Option<Receipt> {
    . . .
  }
}
```

In this example, we are defining a `Person` object that is defined by its name and can optionally have an address associated with it. The address is optionally associated with it because we may not know the person's address when the person is created. We will know the address in the future, so we provide a method to set the address on the person when we know it. Providing "setter" methods is a fairly common programming idiom found in object-oriented languages, so programmers coming from that paradigm would be likely to reach for it in this case. Additionally, we want to be able to mail a package to the person. To mail a package, we need to have the person's address, but that address may not have been defined (it may be `None`), so we have to deal with the fact that we could not deliver it and return an optional `Receipt` to encode the fact that the programmer had not fully specified everything to deliver the package. How do we expect this code to be used?

```
let mut p = Person::new("John Doe");
p.set_address(Address::new("123 John Doe Lane"));
p.mail_package().unwrap();
```

If we write the code in the correct order, our package gets delivered and the unwrap succeeds because our address was set before we tried to mail the package. However, the API we have defined is fragile because it allows us to write code like the following:

```
let mut p = Person::new("John Doe");
p.mail_package().unwrap();
// Boom!
```

So, in the prior code snippet, the `Person` object is in a partially created state from the point-of-view of the `mail_package` method. We have to handle the fact that, at run time, `mail_package` can fail. However, for a properly constructed object, the `mail_package` method can never fail. We can fix this API issue with the Builder pattern.

The Builder pattern is a design pattern that generalizes the construction of an object. Put simply, using the Builder pattern introduces an intermediate object whose sole purpose is to gather up all the state needed to construct the complete object. Given that description, let us reframe our example in terms of the Builder pattern:

```
struct Person {
  name: String,
  addr: Address,
}

impl Person {
 pub fn mail_package(&self) -> Receipt {
    . . .
  }
}

struct PersonBuilder {
  name: String,
  addr: Option<Address>,
}
```

```
impl PersonBuilder {
  pub fn new(name: &str) -> Self {
    PersonBuilder { name: name.into(), addr: None }
  }
  pub fn set_address(mut self, addr: Address) -> Self {
    self.addr = Some(addr);
    self
  }
  pub fn create(self) -> Option<Person> {
    match self.addr {
      None => None,
      Some(addr) => Some(Person { name: self.name, addr: addr })
    }
  }
}
```

The first thing to notice is that it takes more code to implement the Builder pattern because we have a separate object, the `PersonBuilder`, that instantiates our `Person`. Secondly, our `Person` does not have any optional fields in it and the `mail_package` method can no longer fail, because the `address` field is always there. This is good because the users of the `Person` object never have to concern themselves with whether the object they are using is valid or not; it is always in a fully constructed state, able to send packages out. In fact, now our `Person` object, as it is currently defined, can be completely immutable.

But, have we not just moved the problem? In a way, yes, we have. The users of the `PersonBuilder` object must concern themselves with whether the address has been provided to the `PersonBuilder` before trying to instantiate a `Person`. However, this isolates the potential for mistakes to just the construction of the `Person` object; we can then use that `Person` object anywhere else without concern over whether it is valid or not. Additionally, it makes all of the code associated with the `Person` object easier to reason out since, by using the Builder pattern, we are specifying that the `Person` object is complete everywhere that it is used.

We have seen how the Builder pattern can let us isolate the error-prone portion of constructing objects to provide pristine, valid objects for use. However, the Builder pattern also allows us to emulate optional constructor arguments for objects. This is useful whenever there are many different ways to create an object. One way that crops up often in programming is dealing with the many different ways we can open a file.

## Open Options Builder

There are many different ways we can open a file. The simplest way would be to just open the file for reading. Or, we could open the file only for writing. Perhaps, you want to open the file for both reading and writing. For just this small subset of options, we could possibly come up with an API like this:

```
enum OpenOptions {
  Read,
  Write,
  ReadWrite,
}
fn open(name: &str, options: OpenOptions) -> File {}
```

This does not seem unreasonable. We can pass in how we want to open the file as an enum and simply create variants for each different way we want to open the file. This method falls apart, though, when you begin to consider the other ways you can open a file. Let us take a look at a few:

- Read Only
- Read and Write
- Write Only
- Write Only and Create
- Read, Write and Create
- Write Only, Create, and Truncate
- Read, Write, Create, and Truncate

The list can go on, adding other options and other combinations of the existing options, but you get the idea. Each option can generally be combined with every other option, giving $2^N$ combinations of options. We do not want to create an enum that large since handling all of those options in code would be lengthy and it would be difficult for the user of such an API to find the correct variant that needs to be passed in.

In the C file open API, each option is handled as a bit in a bit mask. A straight Rust conversion of the C API would look something like this:

```
const READ: u32 = 1;
const WRITE: u32 = 2;
```

```
const CREATE: u32 = 4;
const TRUNCATE: u32 = 8;
fn open(name: &str, options: u32) -> File {}
```

By bitwise-ORing our option constants together, you can have complete flexibility in how you specify how to open the file. There is a cost, though; you lose type safety by following the C API so closely. By using the above API, the type system cannot prevent you from calling `open` by passing in `0xffff_ffff` for your options. With the above API, you would be setting bits in the bit mask that are undefined, leading to errors that must be checked at run-time.

The Rust standard library uses the Builder pattern to solve this problem with the `OpenOptions` builder. Let us take a look at how the `OpenOptions` builder solves this issue:

```
impl OpenOptions {
  fn new() -> OpenOptions {..}
  fn read(&mut OpenOptions, bool) -> &mut OpenOptions {..}
  fn write(&mut OpenOptions, bool) -> &mut OpenOptions {..}
  fn create(&mut OpenOptions, bool) -> &mut OpenOptions {..}
  fn truncate(&mut OpenOptions, bool) -> &mut OpenOptions {..}
  fn open(OpenOptions, &str) -> Result<File>
}

let file = OpenOptions::new()
    .write(true)
    .create(true)
    .open("foo.txt");
```

The `OpenOptions` builder has methods of specifying whether the file has read, written, created or truncated permissions when opened. By default, the `new` method creates an `OpenOptions` structure with none of those flags set. You can choose which combinations of flags you want to have set, just like bitwise-ORing the flags together in the C-like API example. Unlike the C-like API, the `OpenOptions` builder restricts the flags so that only valid options may be set; i.e., you cannot pass other flags in because the flags are explicitly defined in the Builder structure.

# RESOURCE ACQUISITION IS INITIALIZATION (RAII)

With the Builder pattern, we have seen ways to ensure that an object is always valid once it is created. However, this only covers half of the lifetime of an object. How can we handle the case where, instead of finishing construction of an object, we have a method that begins the destruction of an object such that the object becomes invalid before it goes out of scope? To solve this issue, we can generalize the Builder pattern to fully implement the Resource Acquisition is Initialization (RAII) pattern. Before we talk further about RAII, let us take a look at an example that demonstrates the object becoming invalid before it goes out of scope by looking at a C-like API for manipulating files.

```
let mut fp = open("filename.txt").unwrap();
let data = fp.read_all().unwrap();
fp.close();
// What happens here?
let more_data = fp.read_all().unwrap();
```

In this example, we have a simple file API that allows us to open a file for reading, read the data from the file, and close the file. Both opening and reading from the file can possibly return an error, so, for brevity's sake, we simply unwrap instead of handling the error here. After we have read all of the data from the file, we close the file. However, the file object stored in `fp` is still live, so we can call `read_all` on the `fp` after closing the file. While the file object is still live, it is no longer valid because we have closed the file. We will recognize the error with this API — the `read_all` method will return an error stating that the file was no longer open. However, we can only recognize that error at run time. Preferably, we could come up with an API that would prevent the error using the type system so that we can recognize the error with the compiler instead of with testing. The RAII pattern lets us solve the problem using the type system.

With the RAII pattern, we want to create an object that is valid for its entire lifetime. So, when the object first becomes live, it is completely valid for use. With RAII, the object must stay valid for use until it goes out of scope. With that concept, we can reframe our example code like the following:

```
let data = {
  let mut fp = open("filename.txt").unwrap();
  fp.read_all().unwrap()
};
// Compiler error because fp is not in scope
let more_data = fp.read_all().unwrap();
```

In this example, we are tying the validity of the file object to its lifetime. So, the file is opened when the file object is returned from the open function and the file is closed when the file object goes out of scope; there is no explicit close method. With no explicit close method, the programmer can never cause the file object to become invalid through programmer action. Furthermore, we are protected against accidentally trying to call `read_all` on the file object after it has been closed because the close only happens when the file object goes out of scope, leading the compiler to recognize the error at build time instead of run time.

Rust provides a trait that enables the RAII pattern – the `Drop` trait. The `Drop` trait provides a single method, `drop`, that is implicitly called when objects go out of scope. The `Drop` trait looks like the following:

```
pub trait Drop {
  fn drop(&mut self);
}
```

While very simple, the `Drop` trait allows us to define our own objects that follow the RAII pattern. Let us look in depth at how a simple file API looks when we implement the `Drop` trait for it.

```
struct File;
impl File {
  pub fn open(name: &str) -> File { .. }
  pub fn read_all(&mut self) -> Vec<u8> { .. }
  fn close(&mut self) { .. }
}
impl Drop for File {
  fn drop(&mut self) {
    self.close()
  }
}
```

In our example, we still have public methods that allow us to open up a file and read the data from the file. However, our close function is private. Instead of allowing consumers of the file to close it explicitly, we implement the `Drop` trait on the File object and call `close` when the File is dropped. If we so chose, we could have eliminated the private `close` function completely and simply hooked its implementation into the `Drop` trait implementation.

While the RAII pattern is useful in preventing the use of a partially-destroyed object, the RAII pattern also prevents the programmer from forgetting to clean up resources. In the case of our File API, our new API prevents the user from forgetting to close the file when they are finished with it. Instead, the file is implicitly closed when the file object goes out of scope.

The Rust standard library uses the RAII pattern in many places. Let us look at a few places where the standard library uses the RAII pattern:

| Type | Acquire | Drop |
|---|---|---|
| `File` | open or create file | closes the file |
| `UdpSocket` | bind to a socket address | closes the socket |
| `TcpStream` | `connect` or `TcpListener::accept` | closes the connection |
| `MutexGuard` | `Mutex::lock` or `Mutex::try_lock` | unlocks the mutex |
| `Rc` | `Rc::new` or `Rc::clone` | decrements the refcount |

While we have defined our own, simple file API, the standard library uses the RAII pattern to handle closing files. A file can be opened through the `File::open` or `File::create` methods, which creates a new `File` object. When that `File` object is dropped, the file is closed. The standard library also uses the RAII pattern to track the state of UDP and TCP network sockets. A `UdpSocket` object is created when the socket is bound to an address using the `UdpSocket::bind` function, and the socket is closed when the `UdpSocket` is dropped. Likewise, the `TcpStream` is created when either a connection is made using the `TcpStream::connect` method or a connection is accepted by calling the `TcpListener::accept` method. The connection is closed when dropped.

The RAII pattern can do more than just close files or connections, though. It applies any time you wish to clean up some resource when the object goes out of scope. With a mutex, we want to deterministically limit the lifetime to which a lock is held. Using RAII, we can tie the lifetime to which the lock is held to the lifetime of the `MutexGuard` object. A `MutexGuard` is created when the mutex is locked using `Mutex::lock` or `Mutex::try_lock`. When the `MutexGuard` is dropped, the mutex is unlocked.

As a final example, consider a reference counted (refcounted) smart pointer like the `Rc` object. A refcounted smart pointer keeps a reference count to an object so that the object can be shared among several instances of the pointer. When the smart pointer is created using `Rc::new`, the refcount is initialized with 1. Cloning the smart pointer increments the refcount because there are now multiple pointers that reference the same object. When the `Rc` object goes out of scope and is dropped, the drop method decrements the refcount on the object, ultimately freeing it if it drops to 0. In this case, the resource that is managed by the RAII pattern is the refcount and the decision to free the object when the refcount is 0.

## TYPE-SAFE STATE MACHINES

In terms of the Builder pattern, we have discussed preventing an object from existing in a partially created state by introducing a second object, the builder, to construct the object fully before operations can be done on it. Then, we followed that up with a discussion on the RAII pattern which prevents an object from existing in a partially destructed state by tying the releasing of resources to the liveness of the object itself through the `Drop` trait. Both of these patterns aim to enforce, through the static type system, that the only methods that can be called on the objects are ones that are completely valid at the point in time that they are called. That is, both of these patterns aim to enforce that methods on the objects should not need to return an error due to programmer error. However, neither the Builder pattern nor the RAII pattern can prevent the miscalling of methods when your object can have different internal states where some methods are only valid in specific states, like you would see with a state machine implementation. Let us take a look at a specific example to see what we mean.

In this example, we are going to describe a simple state machine to drive an ATM. In our ATM, we are only going to support a few operations: inserting our ATM card, entering our PIN, choosing to withdraw cash, and dispensing the amount of cash that we chose. Figure 8-1 shows a state transition diagram that describes how the methods should be called to move our ATM between the different states.

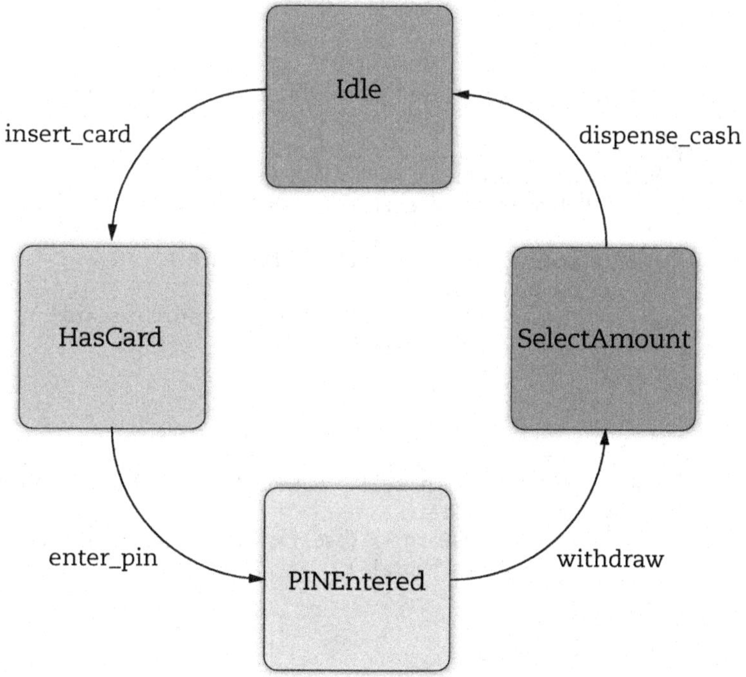


**Figure 8-1:** Simple state machine for an ATM

Our example ATM starts in the `Idle` state and, when it receives the `insert_card` message, it transitions into the `HasCard` state. Once in the `HasCard` state, the ATM can accept PINs, so the ATM will allow the `enter_pin` message to be received. Once the ATM transitions to the `PINEntered` state, we can choose an ATM operation, in this case, to withdraw money. That transitions us to our `SelectAmount` state, where we can `dispense_cash`. Note that the messages are really only valid when the ATM is in a particular state. For instance, the ATM will not allow dispense_cash to be called from the HasCard state, because the user has not authenticated with a PIN and has not selected to withdraw money.

We can simply represent the state machine as follows:

```
pub enum State {
    Idle, HasCard, PINEntered, SelectAmount,
}

pub struct ATM {
    state: State,
    cash: usize,
}
```

State transitions are handled as methods on the ATM object:

```
impl ATM {
    pub fn new(amount: usize) -> ATM {
        ATM { state: State::Idle, cash: amount }
    }
    pub fn insert_card(&mut self) -> &mut ATM {
        match self.state {
            State::Idle => { self.state = State::HasCard; },
            _ => unreachable!(),
        }
        self
    }

    pub fn enter_pin(&mut self) -> &mut ATM {
        match self.state {
            State::HasCard => { self.state = State::PINEntered; },
            _ => unreachable!(),
        }
        self
    }

    pub fn withdraw(&mut self) -> &mut ATM {
        match self.state {
            State::PINEntered => { self.state = State::SelectAmount; },
            _ => unreachable!(),
        }
        self
    }

    pub fn dispense_cash(&mut self, amount: usize) -> &mut ATM {
```

```
        match self.state {
            State::SelectAmount => { self.state = State::Idle; self.cash =
amount; },
            _ => unreachable!(),
        }
        self
    }
}
```

In the transition methods, we match on the current state of the ATM and, if the ATM is in the correct state for the method, then we perform the action and transition to the next state in the state machine. Notice, however, that if we are not in the correct state, we must do something about it. We could choose to return an error from the state transition function and force every caller to handle the possibility that the functions were called out of order, or we could simply panic by using the `unreachable!` macro. In this case, we use the `unreachable!` macro because a properly implemented caller will not call methods out of order.

We can walk through the state machine easily by chaining the calls together:

```
let mut atm = ATM::new(100);
atm.insert_card()
   .enter_pin()
   .withdraw()
   .dispense_cash(25);
```

We create a mutable ATM instance and return a mutable reference to the ATM at the end of each method, which allows us to chain the method calls together. However, the compiler does not prevent us from writing the following code (although it will panic at runtime):

```
let atm = ATM::new(100);
atm.dispense_cash(25); // ERROR: unreachable!
```

There is something unsatisfying about deferring those checks to run-time, though. We would like to be able to use our strong type system to give us a bit more help and prevent us from calling the methods out of order on our ATM. What if there was a way that we could encode our state machine such that the functions to transition to the next state were only available when we were in a state where they were valid? What would that look like?

We could create distinct types for each of our states and encode the valid state transitions as functions implemented on those types. Reframing our ATM state machine would look like this:

```
pub mod atm {
    pub struct Idle { cash: usize }
    pub struct HasCard { cash: usize }
    pub struct PINEntered { cash: usize }
    pub struct SelectAmount { cash: usize }
    pub fn new(amount: usize) -> Idle {
        Idle { cash: amount }
    }
    impl Idle {
        pub fn insert_card(self) -> HasCard {
            HasCard { cash: self.cash }
        }
    }
    impl HasCard {
        pub fn enter_pin(self) -> PINEntered {
            PINEntered { cash: self.cash }
        }
    }
    impl PINEntered {
        pub fn withdraw(self) -> SelectAmount {
            SelectAmount { cash: self.cash }
        }
    }
    impl SelectAmount {
        pub fn dispense_cash(self, amount: usize) -> Idle {
            Idle { cash: self.cash - amount }
        }
    }
}
```

In this example, we created a module for the ATM just to group the state types together. Each state type contains the information needed to track the ATM; in this case, we are tracking the amount of cash that the ATM has in it. Creating a new ATM is as simple as providing a function in the module that takes the amount of cash and produces the `Idle` state, since that is the state in which all new ATMs should start. Back in our state-transition diagram, there was only one valid state transition out of the `Idle` state and into another state — the `insert_card` state transition function would move the ATM into the `HasCard` state. To implement that with our "one type per state" example, we are providing an implementation of our `Idle` state that has a single function, the `insert_card` function. That function consumes the current state by taking `self` by ownership so that the current state cannot live on after calling the state transition. Finally, the `insert_card` function returns the new state, the `HasCard` type. The other state-transition functions for the other types are implemented similarly according to the state-transition diagram.

We can walk through the state machine easily by chaining the calls together:

```
let atm = atm::new(100);
atm.insert_card()
   .enter_pin()
   .withdraw()
   .dispense_cash(25);
```

Since we are returning the new state at the end of each method, Rust knows the type-through-type inference and allows us to chain the method calls together.

```
let atm = atm::new(100);
atm.dispense_cash(25); // ERROR: method not found
```

Now, when we accidentally make a call to a method that is not allowed at this point in the state machine, we get a compile time error letting us know what happened.

We have introduced a new issue, though. In making the valid state transitions enforced at compile-time, we have restricted the use of our state machine to simple, chained calls as in the example above. We cannot keep our state machine as a member of another data structure because we change the type of the state machine at every state transition:

```
struct Foo {
  state: atm::Idle,
}
let mut foo = Foo { state: atm::new(100) };
// ERROR: types differ here
foo.state = foo.state.insert_card();
```

When we try to store our new state back into the `Foo` data structure, we cannot because `insert_card` returns a `HasCard` type and the type of the `state` variable is the `Idle` type. If only there was a way to store several different types, or variants, into a single variable. Oh wait, there is!

To add that run-time flexibility once again, we can wrap our state machine back up into an enum like this:

```
enum State {
  Idle(atm::Idle),
  HasCard(atm::HasCard),
  PINEntered(atm::PINEntered),
  SelectAmount(atm::SelectAmount),
}

struct Foo {
  state: State,
}

#[derive(Debug)]
enum Msg { InsertCard, EnterPin, Withdraw, Dispense(usize) }
fn get_msg() -> Msg { unimplemented!(); }

let mut foo = Foo {
  state: State::Idle(atm::new(100))
};

foo.state = match (get_msg(), foo.state) {
  (Msg::InsertCard, State::Idle(st)) =>  State::HasCard(st.insert_card()),
  (Msg::EnterPin, State::HasCard(st)) => State::PINEntered(st.enter_
pin()),
  (Msg::Withdraw, State::PINEntered(st)) => State::SelectAmount(st.
withdraw()),
  (Msg::Dispense(x), State::SelectAmount(st)) => State::Idle(st.dispense_
cash(x)),
  (msg, _) => response("invalid state for {:?}", msg),
};
```

You might be thinking, "What did we gain by encoding the state as separate types if we just have to wrap everything up again with an enum and match on it?". What we gained was a degree of safety. In this model, we are simulating the interaction of a state machine with the outside world by having the `get_msg` function provide us with a message that corresponds to a state transition that should happen. We know, for instance, that the `InsertCard` message should only come in to an ATM in the `Idle` state. If we get that message in that state, we can call the `insert_card` method on the underlying state type to transition us to the following state. If we receive an invalid message, we can handle it appropriately by responding to the outside world with an error message. Receiving an invalid message is not a programmer error, but rather a user error, so it is appropriate to respond with an error message. The type system prevents us from making a programmer error by preventing us from calling, for example, the `pin_entered` method when we receive an `InsertCard` message.

## KEY TAKEAWAYS

- The Builder pattern can be used to ensure that constructed objects are completely valid for all of the methods that might be called on them.
- The RAII pattern can be used to tie the lifetime of a resource to the lifetime of the object that represents it. It prevents objects from referring to invalid resources and the program from forgetting to clean up resources when they are through using them.
- The type-safe state machine pattern can be used to ensure that the programmer does not incorrectly transition a state machine to invalid states or use data that is not valid in the current state.

9

# Writing Tested Code

Everyone likes to think that they write perfect code the first time. Rust even makes it easier to write correct code since its strong type system eliminates whole classes of errors such as buffer overflows and use-after-free issues. However, there are always logical errors that can creep into code written by the best-intentioned developer. Who has not inverted the logic of a test or returned the wrong value out of a function? While Rust cannot provide implicit protections for those types of bugs, Rust does integrate a testing framework into the toolchain that makes it easy for developers to write test functions.

If you are only writing code for your own use, you can probably get away with just writing unit tests to make sure that individual functions are written correctly. However, if you are writing code that is being shared with others (perhaps you are publishing a crate on `crates.io`), then you may want to provide more types of tests such as integration tests that test the boundaries between your modules, documentation tests that verify that the examples you provide in your documentation is correct, or benchmark tests that assist you in performance testing. As we will explore in this chapter, Rust's test framework supports developers in writing all of these types of tests.

To demonstrate how Rust assists you in writing tests, we will first walk through an easy-to-understand data structure API for a minimum binary heap that lives in a fictional `binheap` crate and use that as a structure on which we can hang our tests.

## A MINIMUM BINARY HEAP

In computer science, a minimum heap is a tree-like data structure that satisfies the heap property – given a tree, the parent of the tree has a strictly smaller value than the children of that parent. But what does the heap property actually mean? Well, take a minimum binary heap, for example. A minimum binary heap is a binary tree structure where a parent can have 0, 1, or 2 children and the value of each child node is strictly less than the value of the parent node. However, a minimal binary heap is only partially sorted — while a binary search tree is absolutely ordered – meaning that the order of insertion into the tree does not affect the order of the tree and a depth-first traversal of the tree will produce the contents of the tree in order, the same does not hold for a minimal binary heap. Only upon extraction from the heap will you produce an absolute ordering of the contents of the heap.

Why would you want to use a heap, then? What good is a partially-ordered tree? Typically, a heap is used to implement a priority queue. In a priority queue, the absolute order of the queue does not matter. Instead, we always want to extract the item with the lowest priority from the queue. So, why would we want to take the extra cycles keeping the tree absolutely ordered when all we care about is that at the root of the tree is the minimum value? A minimum binary heap gives us just this property. For example, take a look at Figure 9-1.

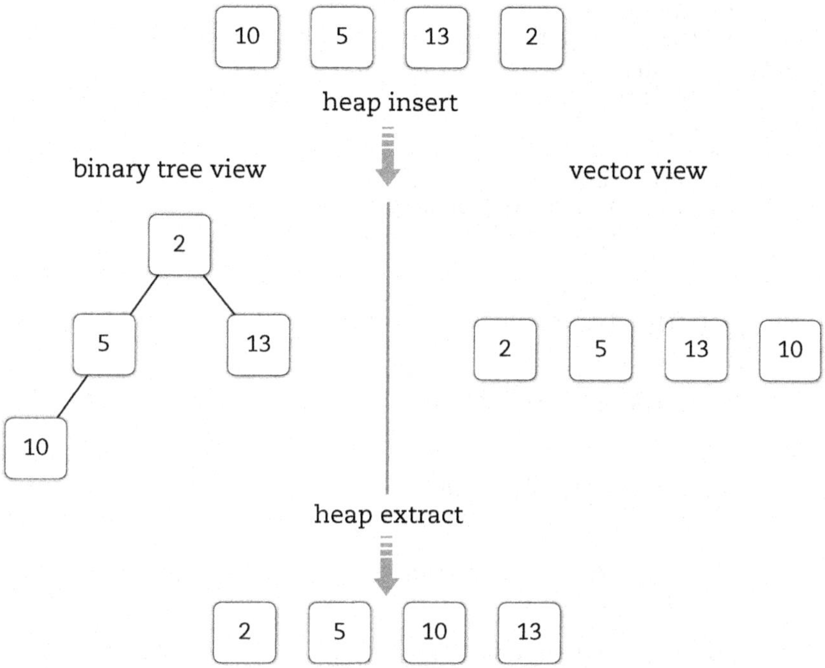


**Figure 9-1:** Insertion into and extraction from a binary heap

At the top of the figure, we have a stream of data that we want to insert into our priority queue (our heap). We insert them into the heap from left to right and produce the two views of our heap – one as a binary tree with a very explicit node structure and another laid out as a vector in memory. Finally, at the bottom of the figure, we can extract each element from the heap, producing the ordered view of the values from least to greatest. From the figure, we can gleam another property from our heap – the absolute root of the tree must be the smallest value in the heap.

How we implement the heap is not relevant for the purposes of this chapter, but we do need to take a look at the interface that the heap provides so that we can test it appropriately.

```
use std::fmt::Debug;
#[derive(Debug, Clone)]
pub struct MinBinaryHeap<T: Debug + Ord> {
    buf: Vec<T>,
}

impl<T: Debug + Ord> MinBinaryHeap<T> {
    pub fn new() -> MinBinaryHeap<T> {
        MinBinaryHeap { buf: Vec::new() }
    }

    fn left(&self, idx: usize) -> Option<usize> {
        ...
    }
    fn right(&self, idx: usize) -> Option<usize> {
        ...
    }
    fn parent(&self, idx: usize) -> usize {
        ...
    }
    pub fn root(&self) -> Option<&T> {
        self.buf.get(0)
    }
    pub fn insert(&mut self, value: T) {
        ...
    }
    pub fn extract(&mut self) -> Option<T> {
        ...
    }
}
```

From this interface, we can determine a few things about the implementation that might be useful for testing purposes. First, we are backing the heap with a simple vector instead of building out a full tree structure. There are non-public methods that let us get at the index of a parent node or, given a parent node, the left and right indices of the children nodes. Since the child nodes may not exist, we return those indices as `Options`. Our public interface consists of a method `root` that allows us to peek at the root, or minimal, value of the heap. Additionally, we have public methods – `insert` and `extract` – that allow us to add and remove values from the heap, respectively.

Given those methods, what are some simple tests that we can add to verify that our heap code is correct? For that matter, how do we even *add* tests to our Rust code?

## SIMPLE UNIT TESTING

The simplest kind of tests that we can add to Rust code is the unit test. A unit test is a test of the smallest possible unit of code. In the case of Rust code, our units are typically individual functions or methods that are implemented on a data structure. To support unit tests, Rust has special markers that you can put on functions to declare that those functions are tests that can be extracted out and run by Cargo when you run the `cargo test` command. When you execute the `cargo test` command, you will see output similar to the following:

```
$ cargo test
    Finished debug [unoptimized + debuginfo] target(s) in 0.0 secs
     Running /Users/jonathan/Documents/Programming Rust/src/chapter_09/
binheap/target/debug/deps/binheap-148856f953ef21b1

running 4 tests
test tests::new_heap_empty ... ok
test tests::insert_adds_value ... ok
test tests::extract_pulls_min_value ... ok
test tests::new_heap_empty_unwrap ... ok
test result: ok. 4 passed; 0 failed; 0 ignored; 0 measured
```

This example test run lists how many test functions were found in the crate, the name of each of the test functions with their pass state, and a summary line at the end. In this test run, our crate has four test functions, and they all passed. Now that we know how to run the unit tests that we want to create, we can demonstrate creating one of those simple unit tests:

```
❶ #[cfg(test)]
  mod tests {
     use super::*;

❷    #[test]
     fn new_heap_empty() {
        let mut heap: MinBinaryHeap<usize> = MinBinaryHeap::new();
        assert_eq!(heap.buf.len(), 0);
        assert_eq!(heap.extract(), None);
     }

     #[test]
     #[should_panic]
     fn new_heap_empty_unwrap() {
         let mut heap: MinBinaryHeap<usize> = MinBinaryHeap::new();
         heap.extract().unwrap();
     }
  }
```

The above code example should live in the same source file as the implementation for the heap. The first interesting bit of the example is marked ❶ – the #[cfg(test)] line. When Cargo builds your test programs, it enables the test feature that can be detected by the #[cfg(test)] line. In this case, the tests module is only compiled in the source file when the test feature is enabled so that test code does not exist in your actual module. Inside of the tests module, we are importing all of the symbols that are defined in the parent module (the rest of the source file). This will let us easily call the functions that we want to test.

The other interesting bit in the example is marked ❷ – the #[test] line. This line tells the Rust compiler that the following function is a test function and should be run as part of the test framework. Inside of that test, we simply create a new MinBinaryHeap for usize values and make sure that it is empty. Since we know that the heap is backed by a vector, we can just assert that the vector has a 0 length. Additionally, for an empty heap, we want to make sure that the extract method correctly returns None, so we use another assertion. In the test, the assert_eq! macro is used to check whether two expressions are equal to each other. If they are not, the macro panics. Rust assumes that a panic corresponds to a failing test. If the test function runs to completion, then the test is considered passing.

We could have re-written those assertions using the general assert! macro like the following:

```
assert!(heap.extract().is_none(), "got unexpected value");
```

The general assert! macro takes any expression as the first argument and, if it evaluates to be true, succeeds. Otherwise, the assert! macro panics and provides the optional second argument as the panic message.

In the second test function we added, there is another directive passed to the compiler, the #[should_panic] directive. That directive inverts Rust's assumption that a panic corresponds to a failing test. If you specify that the test should panic, then a panic corresponds to a passing test and, if the function does not panic, then the test failed. If you are writing tests where you are wanting to make sure that your functions correctly return an error state, consider putting #[should_panic] on the test and simply unwrapping the return. It can make your test code much more concise and easier to understand.

For brevity, we did not show an implementation for unit tests for the insert and extract functions. However, that leads to an interesting problem. How can we test, in general, that those methods are doing the right thing? In a unit test, we can create several contrived test cases that will push at the boundary conditions of our functions, but how can we be sure that we are really covering all of our bases? What if, instead of writing test cases, we simply tested that our functions generally met the requirements they are supposed to implement? We can do that with property-based unit testing.

## PROPERTY-BASED UNIT TESTING

The main idea behind property-based testing is to make general assertions about your code by writing property functions that will succeed when your code is valid. Then, you use a property-testing library to automatically generate test cases and run them against your properties to ensure that they hold. The most well-known library for property-based testing is QuickCheck — a Haskell library for automatically generating test cases. QuickCheck has been ported to many programming languages, including Rust. We will use the quickcheck crate to generate heap test cases by implementing the Arbitrary trait for our data structure.

```
extern crate quickcheck;
use quickcheck::{Arbitrary, Gen};
impl<T: Arbitrary + Debug + Ord> Arbitrary for MinBinaryHeap<T> {
    fn arbitrary<G: Gen>(g: &mut G) -> Self {
        let mut src: Vec<T> = Vec::arbitrary(g);
        let mut arb = Self::new();
        for value in src.drain(..) {
            arb.insert(value);
        }
        arb
    }
}
```

The example code above would be included in our tests modules in the crate source file. In it, we are pulling in the Arbitrary and Gen traits. The Arbitrary trait is used to specify that the data structure can be automatically generated (that we can produce an arbitrary instance of the data structure). The Gen trait represents a generator — a trait that produces random values and can be used to help generate our Arbitrary values. In addition to these two traits, the quickcheck crate provides implementations of the Arbitrary trait for many types in the standard library, including the primitives, vectors, strings, maps, tuples, and even Option and Result types. That makes our implementation for MinBinaryHeap<T> simple, since we can create an Arbitrary Vec<T> and populate our MinBinaryHeap from that. Now that we have a way to generate arbitrary heaps, what can we do with them?

The quickcheck crate provides a handy macro, called quickcheck!, to let us easily define properties that we want to test. But, which properties should we choose? To answer that, let us go back to our definition of the minimum binary heap. One of the properties of a minimum binary heap is that, for every heap, the root value of the heap should be the absolute minimum value of the data structure. So, let us encode that property as a function.

```
quickcheck! {
  fn prop_root_is_minimum_value(xs: MinBinaryHeap<usize>) -> bool {
    let min = xs.buf.iter().min();
    match (min, xs.root()) {
      (Some(min), Some(root)) => min == root,
      (_, None) => true,
      (None, _) => unreachable!(),
    }
  }
}
```

There are a few pertinent features worth exploring here. First, note that our property test is simply a normal function, declared inside of the quickcheck! macro. The function takes a MinBinaryHeap<usize>, which is a type that has Arbitrary implemented on it (since MinBinaryHeap<T> implements Arbitrary as does the primitive usize), and returns bool (whether or not the property is met for the passed in data structure). When the tests are run, the quickcheck library will execute the property function on up to 100 arbitrary instances of the heap and verify that the property passes. If the property fails, the library will attempt to shrink the generated data structure to find the minimum failing test case and will print that out for you.

Looking further at the example, the property is fairly simple. We peek at the interior buffer and get the minimum value of the buffer using the min iterator consumer. Then, we peek at the root value using our public root method. If the root value matches the minimum value, we succeed.

We can take a look at another example property to give you an idea of the types of properties that are useful to define. One thing we want to determine is whether or not the `insert` function is producing valid heaps. Since we are using `insert` in our definition of `Arbitrary`, we should really validate it. According to our heap definition, for every sub-tree in our heap, the parent of the sub-tree must be strictly less than either of its children. We can encode that into a property.

```
fn prop_is_heap(xs: MinBinaryHeap<usize>) -> bool {
  for idx in 0..xs.buf.len() {
    let current = &xs.buf[idx];
    // If there is a right child
    if let Some(right) = xs.right(idx) {
      // It must be larger than the current value
      if current > &xs.buf[right] {
        return false;
      }
    }
    // If there is a left child
      if let Some(left) = xs.left(idx) {
      // It must be larger than the current value
      if current > &xs.buf[left] {
        return false;
      }
    }
  }
  true
}
```

The type of this function is identical to the previous one; it is a function from a `MinBinaryHeap<usize>` to a `bool`. Once again, we exploit the fact that this is a unit test and that we know the implementation details of the data structure to walk every value in the interior vector. Each value in the vector is the parent of a sub-tree, so we check to see if the sub-tree has child nodes. If child nodes exist, we ensure that the values of the child nodes are larger than the value of the parent. If all of the children are larger than all of the parents, then the property passes. Otherwise, it fails.

The power of property-based testing is that we are thinking up logical properties that must hold for the data structure to be valid, instead of trying to think up specific test cases that might show that our properties hold. We are relying on the computer to do what computers do well — do the brute-force computation of generating test cases while we expend programmer-time thinking at a higher level and encoding the invariants in code that we already expect our data structure to meet based on its requirements.

After spending time writing basic unit tests as well as enough property-based tests that we feel confident that our data structure is implemented correctly, we need to make sure that others can use the data structure the way we intend it to be used. We can accomplish that with integration testing.

## INTEGRATION TESTING

Where unit tests are meant to test small units of code, integration tests are meant to be more general. Traditionally in Rust, a unit test will test only code that is defined in the same file that contains the unit test. But how can you test interactions between modules? How can you ensure that you made all of your public APIs and data structures actually public? You can write integration tests to make sure that your API can be used as intended.

Let us add an integration test to verify our public API for the heap data structure.

```
// this code lives in tests/lib.rs
extern crate binheap;
extern crate rand;
use rand::{thread_rng, sample};

#[test]
fn it_works() {
    let mut rng = thread_rng();
    let data = sample(&mut rng, 1..1000, 100);
    let mut heap = binheap::MinBinaryHeap::new();

    // build up our heap
    for x in &data {
        heap.insert(*x);
    }

    let mut old: Option<usize> = None;
    loop {
        // extract each value
        let new = heap.extract();
```

```
        if new.is_none() {
            break;
        }

        // and ensure older value is smaller than
        // newer one
        if let Some(old) = old {
            if let Some(new) = new {
                assert!(old < new);
            }
        }

        old = new;
    }
}
```

There are a few interesting bits to this example. First, note that we are not putting the test case inside of an existing source file in our crate. Rather, we are putting the integration tests inside of a file in the `tests` directory. Since the integrations tests do not live as a part of the crate, we have to import the crate using the `extern crate binheap` syntax. Since we have to import the crate, we only have access to public functions, public data structures, and public fields, just like a consumer of our library would.

In this integration test, we are verifying that we can create a heap, insert many random values into it, and remove them, in order, from smallest to largest. This workflow, while contrived for a test, is roughly how we would expect an end-user of the crate to use the API.

## DOCUMENTATION TESTING

Closely related to integration testing is the idea of making sure that the examples that you have documented in your API documentation always compile and work properly. Rust has integrated support for generating documentation, but it also has built-in support for extracting source code from your documentation markup, compiling it, and running it as a documentation test.

In the following code example, we have very simply documented the `extract` method for our `MinBinaryHeap` structure. In it, we provide a simple description of the method followed by a block of example code that uses the method.

```
/// Extract the minimum value from the heap.
///
/// # Examples
///
/// '''
/// use binheap::MinBinaryHeap;
/// let mut heap = MinBinaryHeap::new();
/// for x in vec![42, 5, 13, 2] {
///     heap.insert(x);
/// }
/// let min = heap.extract().unwrap();
/// assert_eq!(min, 2);
/// '''
pub fn extract(&mut self) -> Option<T> { . . . }
```

In the documentation block, we can use standard Markdown markup to insert headings, make text bold, or in this case, add a source block between consecutive ''' markers. In the source block, simply document how the API is meant to be used. In this case, we are building up a simple heap and extracting the smaller value out of it. We are ensuring that we obtained a value by putting the `unwrap` call after the extract and then asserting that the minimum value we got is really the minimum value that we put in the heap. Additionally, you can add multiple source code blocks and they will each be extracted out as separate test cases.

Like all previous tests, you can run the documentation tests using the same `cargo test` command. When they run, a separate section shows up in the test output that looks like the following:

```
   Doc-tests binheap

running 3 tests
test MinBinaryHeap<T>::insert_0 ... ok
test MinBinaryHeap<T>::insert_1 ... ok
test MinBinaryHeap<T>::extract_0 ... ok

test result: ok. 3 passed; 0 failed; 0 ignored; 0 measured
```

In the output, you can see that three documentation tests were extracted from the source code. In this case, the source code had two source code examples associated with the `insert` method and a single example associated with the `extract` method.

# BENCHMARKING

The final type of testing we are going to discuss is slightly different than other types of testing since there is no way to explicitly check for success and failure. Benchmarking your crate is a good way to ensure that the code you wrote is performant. In the case of our example crate, we want to make sure that using our minimum binary heap to find the minimal value is faster than sorting a vector of numbers to find the minimal value. Let us take a look at some example benchmarking code:

```
// benches/bench.rs
#![feature(test)]
extern crate test;
extern crate binheap;
extern crate rand;

#[cfg(test)]
mod tests {
    use rand::{thread_rng, sample};
    use binheap::*;
    use test::Bencher;

    fn gen_sample() -> Vec<usize> {
        let mut rng = thread_rng();
        sample(&mut rng, 1..1000, 100)
    }

    #[bench]
    fn bench_extract_min(b: &mut Bencher) {
        let data = gen_sample();

        b.iter(|| {
            let mut heap = MinBinaryHeap::new();
            for x in &data {
                heap.insert(x);
            }
            heap.root();
        });
    }
}
```

The first thing to notice in the benchmarking code is that it lives in the `benches/` directory and requires the `test` feature gate to be enabled. The test feature gate allows us to access the built-in test module which is used to import the benchmarking data types and functions; unfortunately, we cannot enable the test feature gate using the stable compiler since the test module API has not been completely stabilized by the compiler team – that is, the Rust developers are still trying to ensure that they have gotten the API correct before they agree to fully support it. So, to run benchmarking tests, we will have to run the benchmarks with the nightly compiler. While there is a risk that the benchmark API found in the `test` module of the nightly compiler might change in the future, the `Bencher::iter` function has been fairly stable in the past and being able to run benchmarking tests is too useful to pass up. We can easily run the benchmarking tests with the nightly compiler using `rustup`:

```
$ rustup run nightly cargo bench
running 2 tests
test tests::bench_extract_min ... bench:         725 ns/iter (+/- 549)
test tests::bench_min_iter    ... bench:       1,402 ns/iter (+/- 383)

test result: ok. 0 passed; 0 failed; 0 ignored; 2 measured
```

Running `cargo` using the `rustup` command in this way will allow us to only use the nightly compiler for running benchmarks while using the stable compiler for all other builds.

Getting back to our source example, we can see that benchmark tests are marked with `#[bench]` instead of `#[test]`. Additionally, the benchmark tests all have the following signature: `fn(&mut Bencher)`. The benchmark runner passes in the `Bencher` type to the test. The `Bencher` type exposes a method called `iter` that calls the passed-in closure many times — as many iterations as it takes for the timing per iteration to statistically stabilize. Since it is up to our code to call the `iter` method, we can run as much setup code per test that we need to without the setup code being benchmarked as well — only the code that is run in the `iter` closure is benchmarked.

# KEY TAKEAWAYS

- Testing is an important part of the crate-creation process. Rust makes it easy to integrate unit, integration, and documentation tests into your build process.
- Using the external `quickcheck` crate, you can augment your unit testing with property-based testing, making it easier to generate test cases for verifying the invariants that your code guarantees.
- Rust has unstable support for running benchmark performance tests. It makes it easy to write performance tests, although you will have to run a nightly compiler to use the built-in functionality.

# 10

# Macros

While Rust is a very expressive language for writing software, there are times that coding in Rust just cannot do everything you want to do. Sometimes, you want to extend the language to do something specific, such as create function-like statements that allow you to return early from a function when an error occurs or to accept a variable number of arguments. Or, perhaps you can easily write your code in Rust, but you must write a lot of repetitive, boilerplate, code correctly to get it right. Both of these problems can easily be solved using compile-time code generation techniques, but code generators are typically cumbersome because they require a separate (outside of the Rust build process) compilation step to generate the code.

This is where Rust macros come in. Rust macros are powerful tools for carrying out compile-time code generation. Macros allow you to extend the language in a standard way, making it easy to have the macro expander generate code for you as a part of the normal Rust build process. You can use macros to implement those variable number of argument function-like statements, those early return statements, and those abstractions over boilerplate. In fact, macros are such fundamental parts of the Rust language that you have likely used without realizing it. Several of the features in the standard library, like `assert_eq!`, `try!`, and `print!` are all implemented as macros, provided for you by the Rust developers.

If you are used to macros in languages like C or C++, do not turn away too quickly! The C PreProcessor (CPP) that is used to process macro definitions in C and C++ is a poor substitution for proper macros like we find in Rust. With CPP, you really only get access to blind text substitution. It is easy to trample on variables and have unusual crop up side effects that are due to the macro implementation. A careful programmer can work around all of these issues, but C and C++ macros are difficult to get right.

Rust macros are different. As we will see, Rust macros allow you to operate on the structure of the code itself to produce new, valid syntactic forms that extend the Rust language. This chapter will demonstrate some common use-cases for macros, some approaches to the overall macro design, and some advanced macro-writing techniques.

## A BRIEF INTRODUCTION TO RUST MACROS

One of the first things a compiler does when compiling code is parse it. The Rust compiler first *tokenizes* the code, splitting it into individual words and symbols and then looks at those tokens and constructs an *Abstract Syntax Tree*, also known as an AST.

As the name suggests, an AST is a tree. It represents your code as a tree of nodes with children. For example, the AST for this:

```
let a = b + c + d;
```

Looks like this:

```
LetStatement {
  name: Identifier("a"),
  value: Add(Identifier("b"),
             Add(Identifier("c"),
                 Identifier("d")))
}
```

Or drawn out in Figure 10-1:

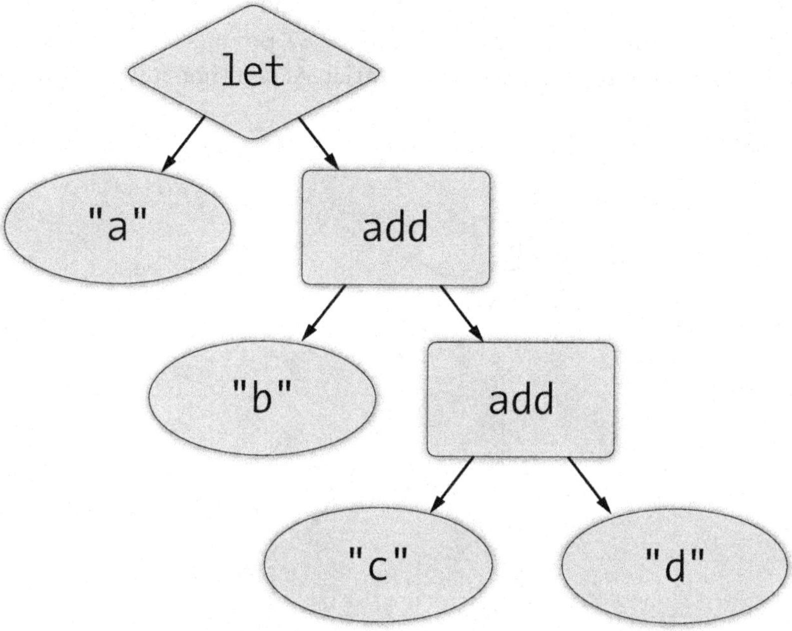


**Figure 10-1:** Abstract syntax tree

Rust macros work with these syntax trees. For example, the AST for this:

```
let x = process!(a, b);
```

looks like Figure 10-2:

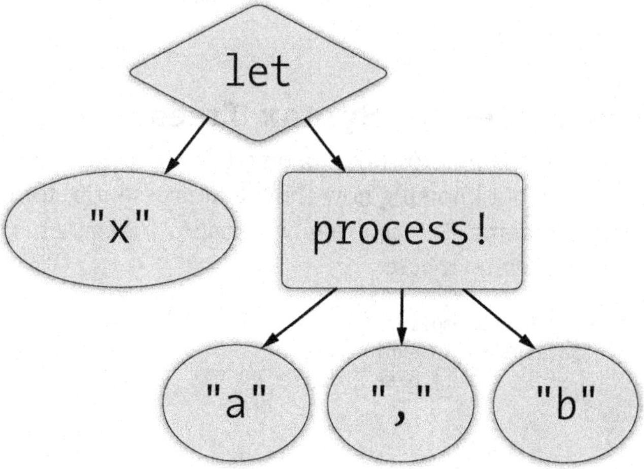


**Figure 10-2:** Abstract syntax tree with macro call

When the compiler expands the **process!** macro, it replaces the part of the tree containing the macro call with the AST produced by the macro. If the **process!** macro multiplies the two variables together, it will expand to Figure 10-3:

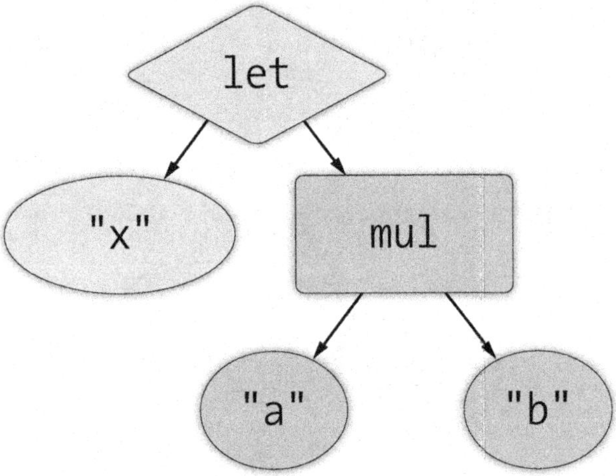


**Figure 10-3:** Macro expansion

The branch of the tree with the **process!** macro call has been completely replaced with the AST for multiplication.

Keen-eyed readers may have spotted that the AST for the macro call had three children, "a", ",", and "b". This is because macros work with *token trees*. Token trees are lists of tokens and sub-trees surrounded by matching delimiters, i.e. (), {}, and [].

## Token Trees to Syntax Trees

Knowing that macros take token trees and return syntax trees is all well and good, but knowing how they do it is essential for understanding and writing macros. To explain how a macro works its magic, let us take a look at the following macro:

```
macro_rules! implies (
  ($a:expr => $b:expr) => (
    if $a { $b } else { false }
  )
);
```

which is used like this:

```
implies!((a >= b && b >= c) => a >= c)
```

The macro defines the implication logical operator, `A => B`, which is true if `A` and `B` are true, but false if `A` is false.

We will take this macro line by line:

```
macro_rules! implies (
```

All macros start with `macro_rules!`, followed by the name of the macro. The body of the macro can be surrounded by braces, `{}`, brackets, `[]`, or parentheses, `()`. While you can use any of the three, common convention suggests using braces when you are creating a block and using parentheses when you are creating an expression.

```
    ($a:expr => $b:expr) => (
```

This line starts a new pattern-matching arm and defines a matcher for the macro. This is the first step in turning a token tree into a syntax tree. A matcher defines what the macro expects and tells the compiler what to do with the tokens in the token tree. Matchers can either match tokens directly, like the `=>` above, or use *fragments* to ask for the token tree to parse according to the fragment specifier. Fragments are identified by `$name:spec`, where `name` identifies the fragment and `spec` is the fragment specifier.

The fragment specifiers are:

- `ident`: matches a single identifier, for example `foo`.
- `path`: a qualified name, for example, `T::Quux`.
- `expr`: a Rust expression, for example, `a + b`.
- `ty`: a type, for example, `Vec<T>`.
- `pat`: a pattern, for example, `(_, Some(t))`.
- `stmt`: a statement, for example, `let x = 1`.
- `block`: a brace-delimited sequence of statements, for example, `{ let a = 1; return a; }`.

- `item`: an item, such as a function, struct or trait definition. For example, `fn foo() { }`.
- `meta`: a "meta item", as found in attributes. For example, `cfg(test)`.
- `tt`: a full token tree.

The next line is:

```
if $a { $b } else { false }
```

This is the expansion of the macro arm and the last step in the process of turning token trees into syntax trees. The expansion produces a special token tree that contains the fragments. The compiler then attempts to parse the token tree, producing the final syntax tree.

## Repetition

The previous macro only took a fixed input – two expressions separated by a =>. Rust macros can, however, support more flexible input via repetition. Here is a macro-using repetition:

```
macro_rules! all (
  ($($e:expr),*) => (
    true $(&& $e)*
  )
);

all!(a, b, c, d)
```

This macro defines a logical and operator over a list of expressions – if all the expressions evaluate to be true, then the macro returns true. When figuring out the expansion of a macro, it can be helpful to draw it out. Figure 10-4 shows the expansion of the macro as each additional portion of the repeated expression is processed:

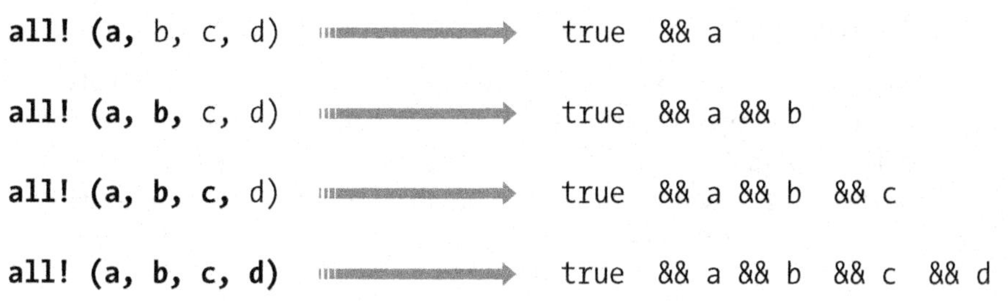


**Figure 10-4:** Repetition in macro expansion

There are a few new things here, but let us start with the matcher. The first new thing is `$(...)`, which wraps a "sub-matcher" to be repeated, the macro will try to repeatedly match using the sub-matcher. The next part is also part of the repetition syntax. Repetitions can match zero-or-more times, or one-or-more times, indicated by the presence of * or +, respectively. Repetitions also have an optional separator that separates each match; we use `,` in our macro, but any token except + or * is valid.

Taking all of that into consideration, we can see that `$($e:expr),*` defines a matcher that matches zero-or-more expressions separated by comma.

In the expansion, we have a similar `$(...)*` that expands the repetition. Since we have `$(&& $e)`, the macro expands each expression to `&&`, followed by the expression. In this example, the expansion name `$e` must be inside of the repetition syntax `$(...)*` because it is only a valid name inside of a repeat block since it was declared in the matcher inside of a repeat block. The expansion also uses a single `true` to serve as the left-hand side of the first expression.

## DESIGNING A MACRO

Being able to read and understand macros is all well and good, but how do you go about writing one? The rest of this chapter will cover just that, starting with the most basic kind of macro, simple pattern abstraction.

## Pattern Abstraction

While macros in general exist to replace repetitive code and boilerplate, pattern-abstraction macros are often the most simplistic. We have already seen one, the `implies!` macro. Pattern abstraction macros take their inputs and place them directly into an expansion, often not using any repetition, or only using basic repetition.

Since they are so simplistic, they are a great place to talk about macro design approaches. First, however, we need a pattern to abstract:

```
let val = match opt_val {
  Some(val) => val,
  None => return None
};
```

This is a common pattern that arises when working with `Option<T>` values. You have some function that needs the value from the `Option<T>`, and will return `None` if it cannot. Put into a function and used multiple times, it looks like this:

```
fn do_stuff(&self) -> Option<i32> {
  let a = match self.get_val("a") {
    Some(a) => a,
    None => return None
  };
  let b = match self.get_val("b") {
    Some(b) => b,
    None => return None
  };
  let c = match self.get_special_val("c", a) {
    Some(c) => c,
    None => return None
  };

  let val = if a {
    b + c
  } else {
    b - c
  };

  Some(val)
}
```

The repetitive nature is obvious here – there is only a small difference between each instance of the pattern. Before we reach for a macro, however, we should look at what other options are available to us.

The first thing to consider is whether or not a function or method could completely replace the pattern here. The answer is no in this case, as the pattern contains `return None`, meaning it influences control flow in the function itself.

The next thing to consider is whether or not there is a different way of writing the same thing, and whether or not that way is acceptable. Here are two alternative ways to write the above function:

```
fn do_stuff(&self) -> Option<i32> {
  if let Some(a) = self.get_val("a") {
    if let Some(b) = self.get_val("b") {
      if let Some(c) = self.get_special_val("c", a){
        let val = if a < 0 {
          b + c
        } else {
          b - c
        };

        return Some(val);
      }
    }
  }
  None
}
```

This uses nested `if lets` instead of early returns. While not too bad, it does demonstrate a phenomenon known as "rightward drift" where your code drifts to the right-hand side of the screen as you nest more control flow.

```
fn do_stuff(&self) -> Option<i32> {
  self.get_val("a").and_then(|a| {
    self.get_val("b").and_then(|b| {
      self.get_special_val("c", a).map(|c| {
        if a < 0 {
          b + c
        } else {
          b - c
        }
```

```
        })
      })
    })
  }
```

This uses the methods `Option::and_then` and `Option::map` which both execute a closure when the value is `Some(T)`, but not when the value is `None`. It suffers a similar problem to the earlier example – rightward drift. The use of closures also complicates control flow, as a `return` inside a closure returns from the closure, not the function.

Now that we have established that a macro is the way we want to go here, we need to decide how we want it to be used. Macros can effectively design their own syntax, so deciding how we want our macro to be used is important, as it influences how we write the macro.

In this case, we only care about a single value, so we want it to be used like this:

```
let val = try_opt!(opt_val);
```

Once we have our usage defined, we can move on to writing the macro itself. Oftentimes, the main challenge here is figuring out what the matcher should look like. Here, we want to accept any expression, so we use an expression fragment:

```
macro_rules! try_opt (
  ($opt:expr) => (
    /***/
  )
);
```

The final part is the expansion. A good way to figure out what should go in the expansion is to write out what you want to expand to, and work backwards.

```
match opt_val {
  Some(val) => val,
  None => return None
}
```

The part that will differ between different macro calls is highlighted above – this is where we will put our fragment in the expansion. Adding that to our macro gives us the completed macro:

```
macro_rules! try_opt (
  ($opt:expr) => (
    match $opt {
      Some(val) => val,
      None => return None
    }
  )
);
```

Now our function looks like this:

```
fn do_stuff(&self) -> Option<i32> {
  let a = try_opt!(self.get_val("a"));
  let b = try_opt!(self.get_val("b"));
  let c = try_opt!(self.get_special_val("c", a));

  let val = if a < 0 {
    b + c
  } else {
    b - c
  };

  Some(val)
}
```

Success! This is a number of lines shorter, and much less repetitive. The pattern we identified has been moved into the macro, meaning that the remaining code is more concise and easier to understand. In fact, this macro is useful enough that it has already been written for you and provided in the `try_opt` crate.

If making code a few lines shorter and removing some repetition is good, how about removing a lot of lines of boilerplate code? Typically, we would use some form of code generation to remove that boilerplate. Rust's macro system can give us a helping hand to hide boilerplate behind new syntax-use code-generation macros.

## Code Generation Macros

Code generation has a long tradition in software development. Not everything can be abstracted into nice, reusable packages, or processed at runtime. Sometimes performance concerns force your hand, other times you may want to leverage the static checking the compiler can give you. In these cases, code generation is the tool of choice.

Code generation generally has two components: the source data and the code generator. The source data can be as simple as a comma-separated table or as complex as binary file format, the code generator then uses that source data to produce source code in the language you're working with. One issue with code generation, however, is that your compiler or interpreter does not know that it is generated code and about the code generator. Therefore, any errors in the generated code are actually errors in the code generator, but figuring out where the error exists can be a challenge.

This is where code generation macros come in – macros that receive data and generate code (often a lot of code). The main advantage of using macros is that the Rust compiler is aware of macros and can often identify errors closer to their real location. They are still limited in that the macro expansion is happening at compile-time and only has the token tree to work with instead of the full program state present at runtime, but for purposes of code generation we can write macros that will work within those limits.

As an example, let us use a set of errors from a fictional database. We could write all of this code by hand, but that gets really repetitive and would lead us to copy and paste snippets of code around, possibly leading to incorrect code. It would be great if we could simply supply the name, the error code, and a description of each error case and have our code generator produce a single C-like `enum` with a value associated with each error value as well as a method to let us get a string description of the error that depends on the error value. We will use the process we laid out earlier, but we will skip writing all of the code out by hand first since that is the exact thing we are trying to avoid doing by using the macro!

The first step, instead, is to decide how we want the macro to look when used. We have three pieces of information for each error and want to make it clear how they fit together. Let us use it like this:

```
db_errors! {
  InvalidQuery,        1, "Query was invalid";
  PermissionDenied,    2, "Permission Denied";
  ConstraintViolation, 3, "Constraint Violation";
}
```

This has the name, the code, and the description separated by commas and each error is terminated with a semicolon. The next step is therefore to write out the matcher for this syntax:

```
macro_rules! db_errors {
  ($($name:ident, $code:expr, $desc:expr;)+) => (
    /***/
  )
}
```

We are using repetition here to match each line. There is no separator for the repetition as each error has a terminating semicolon instead. For the code and description, we use the `expr` fragment specifier as there is no way to specifically match against an integer literal or string literal.

Next, we need to figure out what should go into the expansion. Once again, writing out the result is a good way to see what we need. This is the expansion for just a single error:

```
#[derive(Copy, Clone, Debug)]
pub enum Error {
  InvalidQuery = 1,
}

impl Error {
  pub fn description(&self) -> &str {
    use self::Error::*;
    match *self {
      InvalidQuery => "Query was invalid",
    }
  }
}
```

Again, the parts of the expansion that are provided in the macro call have been highlighted.

Using this as a base, we can write the expansion like this:

```
macro_rules! db_errors {
  ($($name:ident, $code:expr, $desc:expr;)+) => (
    #[derive(Copy, Clone, Debug)]
    pub enum Error {$(
      $name = $code,
    )+}

    impl Error {
      pub fn description(&self) -> &str {
        use self::Error::*;

        match *self {$(
          $name => $desc,
        )+}
      }
    }
  )
}
```

The expansion contains two repetitions: one in the definition of the `enum` and another in the `match` expression. Each error gets its own entry in the `enum` with the corresponding code and its own arm in the `match`.

While this example only has three errors to avoid presenting you with several pages consisting of just code, the more errors you have to work with, the more valuable this is. If you want to add additional functionality to the generated type, you can do so relatively easily by adding a method to the expansion. Adding new error cases is also easy as the macro expansion will automatically include the new entries.

## Custom Derive

Using macros to perform code generation is useful, but how would we write a macro that could implement a trait for us? For the purposes of this discussion, let us consider a trait that will deal with generating updating a message digest with the contents of the data type. Our example trait looks like this:

```
extern crate digest;
use digest::Digest;
pub trait DoDigest<D: Digest> {
    fn update_digest(&self, &mut D);
}

impl<D> DoDigest<D> for String
    where D: Digest
{
    fn update_digest(&self, digest: &mut D) {
       digest.input(self.as_bytes());
    }
}
```

In this example, what the `digest.input(..)` function is doing is not really important; all that is important is that we are calling it on the contents of the `String` to update the message digest. Ideally, given the trait and that implementation of the trait, we would like to create structs that contain strings and have some way to generate the code that will implement the trait for us. The following example shows the type of code we would like to generate:

```
// Given this struct
struct Foo {
    bar: String,
    baz: String,
    quux: String,
}

// Generate this implementation
impl<D> DoDigest<D> for Foo
    where D: Digest,
{
    fn update_digest(&self, digest: &mut D) {
        self.bar.update_digest(digest);
        self.baz.update_digest(digest);
        self.quux.update_digest(digest);
    }
}
```

Since the code for the `update_digest` method is very repetitive for each struct that we want to define, we would like to use a macro to automatically generate the code for us. Our first thought is to define some macro, maybe called `derive_digest`, that we could call on the struct `Foo` like this:

derive_digest!(Foo). This does not work, though. After we have declared the struct Foo, the macro engine no longer contains data on the fields that are inside of the struct. So, we have no way of generating the list of field names for our update_digest function.

One common work-around for that would be do re-iterate the list of field names in the call to the macro. So, we could define a macro that we call as follows: derive_digest!(Foo, { bar, baz, quux }). This is workable and, prior to Rust 1.15, was the only way to solve this problem on stable Rust. However, the solution is very unsatisfying. We have to repeat the list of field names in the macro and, any time you are forced to repeat a list of items, you will eventually miss an item and one of the fields will not get pulled into the digest. Fortunately, Rust 1.15 provided a solution to the issue in the form of Custom Derive syntax.

You may remember that there are several special traits that can automatically be derived for types by using a derive statement immediately before the declaration of the data type such as the following: #[derive(Debug, Clone)]. The Custom Derive functionality provided by Rust 1.15 gives programmers the ability to create procedural macros (e.g. macros that are Rust procedures that act on the Rust syntax tree directly) to create their own derive handlers that allow traits to be automatically derived for types. To implement a custom derive handler for a trait, we need to first create a new crate for the procedural macro, pull in a few helper crates, and generate a little bit of boilerplate:

```
extern crate proc_macro;
extern crate syn;
#[macro_use]
extern crate quote;

use proc_macro::TokenStream;

#[proc_macro_derive(DoDigest)]
pub fn do_digest(input: TokenStream) -> TokenStream {
    let s = input.to_string();
    let ast = syn::parse_derive_input(&s).unwrap();
    let gen = impl_do_digest(&ast);
    gen.parse().unwrap()
}
```

In the above code snippet, we are declaring that we want to use the `do_digest` function to handle the custom derive of `DoDigest`, so that we can place a `#[derive(DoDigest)]` directive in front of a type declaration. Generally, that function is a bit of boilerplate (we could use another macro here if we really wanted to!) that:

- takes the input token stream and converts it to a string,
- parses out the derive input (also known as the type definition that the derive statement is attached to),
- calls our specific handler function to generate a trait implementation, and
- parses the returned tokens into a `TokenStream` for compilation.

All of the magic happens in during the call to our specific handler function, `impl_do_digest`:

```
fn impl_do_digest(ast: &syn::DeriveInput) -> quote::Tokens {
    // part #1
    let name = &ast.ident;
    if let syn::Body::Struct(ref body) = ast.body {
        let field = match *body {
            syn::VariantData::Struct(ref fs) => {
                fs.iter().map(|f| f.ident.as_ref().unwrap().clone())
                         .collect()
            },
            syn::VariantData::Tuple(ref fs) => {
                fs.iter().enumerate().map(|(i, _)| i.into()).collect()
            },
            _ => vec![],
        };
        // part #2
        quote! {
            impl<D> DoDigest<D> for #name
                where D: Digest
            {
                fn update_digest(&self, digest: &mut D) {
           #( self.#field.update_digest(digest); )*
                }
            }
        }
    } else {
        panic!("#[derive(DoDigest) is only defined for structs");
    }
}
```

This function can roughly be split into two portions: the first segment of code takes the syn::DeriveInput data type and walks the data structure, extracting the name of the type and a list of fields found in the struct. For simplicity, we are not allowing the DoDigest trait to be derived for enums (that is left as an exercise for the reader), so we can simply walk the list of named fields in a struct or generate a list of indexes into a tuple.

The second part of the impl_do_digest function takes the extracted name and fields and generates a trait implementation using the quote! macro from the quote crate. The quote! macro uses quasi-quotation to pull the contents of variables in from the surrounding scope and insert them into a token stream using #var-type of syntax very similar to the Rust macro syntax, including support for repetition. So, in this case, our impl_do_digest function creates an implementation of our DoDigest trait for the #name struct and, in the update_digest function, calls update_digest on each #field in the struct. While there is little room here for anything other than a simple example, more complex trait implementations can be done. For more advanced structure parsing and quote generation, see the excellent documentation provided by the syn crate for a complete description of the syn::DeriveInput type and quote crate for a complete description of the quote! macro.

Given a proper implementation of impl_do_digest, this will almost compile. We also need to declare that the do_digest_derive crate is a procedural macro crate, so we need to add the following to the Cargo.toml file:

```
[lib]
proc-macro = true
```

With our custom derive implemented, we can now write code like the following that will derive an implementation for our DoDigest trait:

```
#[macro_use]
extern crate do_digest_derive;
extern crate do_digest;
extern crate digest;

use do_digest::DoDigest;
use digest::Digest;
```

```
#[derive(DoDigest)]
struct Foo {
    bar: String,
    baz: String,
    quux: String,
}
```

# ADVANCED MACROS

Now that we have seen a couple of basic macros and how to approach their design and implementation, we can move onto some more advanced techniques. Rust macros allow you to define multiple matchers for the same macro. Multiple matchers allow you to be extremely flexible new syntax that you are defining. Additionally, by exploiting recursion on parsing token trees, you can define macros with arbitrary nesting depth, which is generally useful when building up domain-specific languages using macros.

## Multiple Matchers

All of the previous macros we have defined have used a single matcher, as that is all they needed. Indeed, most macros only require a single matcher to function. However, macros can have multiple matchers, each one with their own expansion.

Take the following macro for defining a simple bitset. A bitset is a data type where each bit in a word is considered a separate value and more than one bit can be set at a time. Rust enums are not suitable for defining bitsets as they cannot be values other than one of the variants. You can emulate a bitset using a Rust enum and a set data structure; however, for a small number of variants, a bitset is much more efficient to store. You can create a true bitset in Rust with a struct type and constants for each variant.

```
macro_rules! bitset {
  (pub $name:ident : $t:ty {
      $($valname:ident = $val:expr),+ }) => (
    pub struct $name($t);

    $(pub const $valname : $name = $name($val);)+
  );
```

```
    ($name:ident : $t:ty {
        $($valname:ident = $val:expr),+ }) => (
      struct $name($t);

      $(const $valname : $name = $name($val);)+
    );
}
```

Notice that there are two arms. The first one matches pub, the second one does not. This is used to control whether or not the generated type and constants are pub. While both expansions are similar here, this is not required – each expansion can be much greater or smaller than the others.

The main rule for multiple matchers is that the top match wins. In our bitset macro, this does not matter as the two arms cannot match the same pattern; however, it can matter in other cases, as we will see.

```
bitset! {
  pub Sample : usize {
    FOO = 1,
    BAR = 2,
    BAZ = 4,
    QUUX = 8
  }
}
pub struct Sample(usize);
pub const FOO : Sample = Sample(1);
pub const BAR : Sample = Sample(2);
pub const BAZ : Sample = Sample(4);
pub const QUUX : Sample = Sample(8);
```

The previous example usage of the bitset macro shows an expansion of the first arm of the macro. To truly completely make the bitset macro, we would need to define additional operations on the bitset type that gets created, but that is left as an exercise for the reader.

## Recursive Macros

Due to the way macros work, a single matcher cannot match an arbitrary-depth tree. To demonstrate what this means, consider the following expression we want to match:

```
[ [ [ a ] ] ]
```

We want to write a macro to extract that a. One such macro is this:

```
macro_rules! get_a (
  ([[[$a:ident]]]) => ($a)
);
```

This works fine; each pair of [] is matched and the a is matched using an ident fragment. What if we were given this instead:

```
[ [ [ [ a ] ] ] ]
```

With our current macro, we would get this error message:

```
error: expected ident, found [
```

Okay, no problem, we will add another arm to the macro:

```
macro_rules! get_a (
  ([[[[$a:ident]]]]) => ($a);
  ([[[$a:ident]]]) => ($a)
);
```

It has to go above, though, otherwise the macro will attempt to match [a] against $a:ident and give the same error message as before. Hopefully, you can see where this is going – each level requires a new matcher, for zero to four pairs. The macro looks like this:

```
macro_rules! get_a (
  ([[[[$a:ident]]]]) => ($a);
  ([[[$a:ident]]]) => ($a);
  ([[$a:ident]]) => ($a);
  ([$a:ident]) => ($a);
  ($a:ident) => ($a)
);
```

Consider that the expansion and the matchers are very simple in this example – a more complex macro would quickly get out of hand. More importantly, however, is that the depth is still limited to a fixed number – if we wanted to match an expression with five pairs of brackets, we would have to add another arm.

There is a way to avoid this, though. This technique relies on two facts:

1. macros operate on token trees, and
2. one of the fragment specifiers allows you to match on raw token trees.

With those two facts in mind, you can write a macro that can recursively call your macro with the token tree. The `get_a!` macro rewritten to use token trees and recursion looks like this:

```
macro_rules! get_a (
  ([$tree:tt]) => (get_a!($tree)); // (1)
  ($a:ident) => ($a)              // (2)
);
```

To understand how this works, let us step through the expansion of `get_a!([[[a]]])`:

```
   get_a!([[[a]]]) matches (1) $tree = [[a]]
=> get_a!( [[a]] ) matches (1) $tree =  [a]
=> get_a!(  [a]  ) matches (1) $tree =   a
=>           a     matches (2)    $a =   a
```

At each step, one layer of [] is stripped off by arm (1). Once there are no more []s, (2) matches and the recursion stops. This pattern of "recursive case" and "base case" is necessary, so when designing your own recursive macros, you should ensure that you have a clear stopping point.

## Tree Parsing

Now that we know how to use recursion to handle arbitrary-depth token trees, let us put that to use. So far, we have only written macros that take lists, but a more interesting application is defining custom *domain-specific languages*, or DSLs. A DSL is a small language that can be embedded inside of the source language that allows you to solve the problem at hand inside of a specific domain. Without realizing it, you likely write code in a DSL all of the time. The formatting arguments for the `println!` macro comprise a small language specialized for printing objects as strings. Using the Rust macro system, we can create a simple DSL to solve optimization problems much like you would find in a compiler or interpreter system.

Most modern compilers use an intermediate representation of code before generating machine code. This intermediate representation is what is analyzed and modified for optimization. For example, the following code might be the representation for `p += 0`:

```
%x = load %p
%y = add %x, 0
     store %y, %p
```

Now, it is clear that `p += 0` does not do anything, as `x + 0 = x`. An optimizer should be able to remove the `add %x 0`, replacing all uses of `%y` with `%x`. In order to do this, we need to find where this happens. This might be done like this:

```
let function = ...;
for instruction in function.instructions() {
  if let Add(lhs, rhs) = instruction {
    if let Some(0) = lhs.as_const_val() {
      function.replace_uses(instruction, rhs);
    } else if let Some(0) = rhs.as_const_val() {
      function.replace_uses(instruction, lhs);
    }
  }
}
```

So, this loops through all the instructions in a function, finds `Add` instructions and, if one of the operands is zero, replaces the uses of it with the other operand.

This type of pattern-matching is common, and can be more complex than this. A pattern-matching DSL would be more understandable and less error-prone. Let us use the adding-zero case as our motivation:

```
let mut val = undef_value();
vmatch!(instruction = Add 0 val);
```

This macro will return `true` if the match succeeded and assign the left-hand side of the add instruction to `val`, returning false otherwise. We want our macro to be general though, so we should probably use a more complex example to make sure we get what we want:

```
vmatch!(instruction = Add a (Add b (Add c d)))
```

This matches the expression `a + (b + (c + d))`.

So, how do we match this with a macro? Breaking down the `vmatch!` macro call gets us two parts: the pattern we are matching against – `instruction` – and the pattern we are testing. We can start by writing out a part of the matcher like this:

```
macro_rules! vmatch (
  ($val:ident = /* pattern */) => (
    /***/
  )
);
```

This matches the `instruction =` part, but now we have to figure out the matcher for the pattern. From the second example, we can see that we want to nest patterns; that is, we want to match instructions that have operands that match other patterns. As we have already seen, the way to handle nesting is by using token-trees and recursion. We will use a second macro for the patterns, meaning that the `vmatch!` macro looks like this:

```
macro_rules! vmatch (
  ($val:ident = $($p:tt)+) => (
    do_match($val, _pat!($($p)+))
  )
);
```

It expands to a call to a `do_match` function that will run the pattern object produced by `_pat!` against the value. The `_pat!` macro is where the real work is. We want to write a macro that accepts both `Add 0 a` and `Add a (Add b (Add c d))` and expands to something that does what we want. The syntax of these patterns is this:

```
Pat = (Pat)
    | "Add" Pat Pat
    | Ident
    | "0"
```

That is, a pattern, `Pat`, is either the word “Add” followed by two patterns, an identifier, “0”, or parentheses around any of these. Each of these is a separate arm in the macro:

```
macro_rules! _pat (
  // (Pat)
  (($($p:tt)+)) => (_pat!($($p)+));

  // "Add" Pat Pat
  (Add $lhs:tt $rhs:tt) => (
    match_add(_pat!($lhs), _pat!($rhs));
  );

  // Ident
  ($i:ident) => (bind_value(&mut $i));

  // "0"
  (0) => (match_zero())
);
```

Here, match_add, match_zero and bind_value are functions that build a specific pattern. Since this is a recursive macro, we should make sure we have a base case. As it turns out, we have two! Both the Ident and "0" cases halt recursion.

So, what does our motivating example expand to?

```
   vmatch!(instruction = Add 0 val)
=> do_match(instruction, _pat!(Add 0 val))
=> do_match(instruction,
            match_add(_pat!(0), _pat!(val)))
=> do_match(instruction,
            match_add(match_zero(),
                      bind_value(&mut val)))
```

The more complex example expands to this (most of the intermediate expansions have been omitted for brevity):

```
   vmatch!(instruction = Add a (Add b (Add c d)))
=> do_match(instruction,
            _pat!(Add a (Add b (Add c d))))
=> do_match(instruction,
            match_add(bind_value(&mut a),
              match_add(bind_value(&mut b)),
                match_add(bind_value(&mut c),
                          bind_value(&mut d)))))
```

In both cases, the macro is much more concise and clear than its expansion. The macro call better conveys the intent of the programmer that would otherwise be unclear, hidden amongst the calls to build the pattern in the first place.

## KEY TAKEAWAYS

- Macros can be used to create new syntactic forms that allow you to abstract away patterns that are not possible with normal functions. Macros can also assist in abstracting away boilerplate code, making code easier to read and write.
- Rust macros are more complex, but more powerful, than the macros from C or C++ that you might be familiar with.

11

# Foreign Function Interface

As great as Rust is, not all software is written in Rust, yet. Until that happens, and when you can just pick a Rust library to suit your needs, Rust provides a foreign function interface, or FFI, to allow Rust to talk to other languages. A "foreign function" is any function that is not written in the native language (Rust).

In the first part of this chapter, we will cover binding to a foreign library and writing a wrapper for it. The second part will cover the opposite – exposing Rust code in a way that allows foreign code to interact with it.

### Using `libc`

Many of the examples in this chapter will be using types from the `libc` crate. This crate is available on `crates.io`, and can be used in your project by adding this to your dependencies:

```
[dependencies]
libc = "0.2"
```

The current version of the `libc` crate as of this writing is `0.2.29`, so specifying `0.2` gives you the latest patch version of the `0.2 libc` API version.

## BINDING TO FOREIGN CODE

As the foreign function interface requires foreign functions to interface with, we will be using the following, fictional, library in this chapter. It is an image-manipulation library for an unspecified file format; we will see how to bind to it in Rust and how to create a safe wrapper over those bindings. The following code shows the declarations for the C data types and function calls that comprise the library.

```
typedef struct image_t image_t;
typedef struct row_t row_t;

typedef enum {
  FORMAT_RGB8,
  FORMAT_RGBA8,
  FORMAT_PALETTE
} format_t;

typedef struct {
  uint16_t width;
  uint16_t height;
  format_t format;
} header_t;

typedef struct {
  char *data;
  unsigned int width;
  unsigned int height;
} block_t;

typedef void (* modify_callback_t)
    (block_t * block, void *user);

// Reads an image from the given file returning an
// opaque pointer representing the image, or NULL if
// an error is encountered.
image_t *read_from_file(const char *name);

// Reads an image from the given pointer returning
// an opaque pointer representing the image, or NULL
// if an error is encountered.
image_t *read_from_memory(const char *data,
                          unsigned int len);

// Frees the data associated with the given image.
// The pointer will not be valid after calling this
// function
```

```
void destroy_image(image_t *image);

// Fills the given 'header' pointer with the header
// data of the image.
// 'header' must be a valid pointer.
void get_header(const image_t *image,
                header_t *header);
// modify the image block-by-block.
// The callback is called with a block of pixels at
// most 'block_width' by 'block_height' in size.
// The 'user' pointer is passed directly to the
// callback.
void modify_image(image_t *image,
                  unsigned int block_width,
                  unsigned int block_height,
                  modify_callback_t cb,
                  void *user);

// Gets the first row in the image
// You must not use the returned pointer after
// calling 'destroy_image'.
const row_t *first_row(const image_t *image);
// Gets the next row in the image
// The 'row' pointer is invalid after calling
// this function.
const row_t *next_row(const row_t *row);
// Gets the data associated with the row.
// Calling 'next_row' will invalidate the pointer
// returned by this function.
const char *row_data(const row_t *row);
```

## Binding Types

Types from C need to be translated into their Rust equivalents. There are four cases: opaque types, structs, enums, and typedefs. Native C types also need to be translated. All primitive types are exposed via the `libc` crate and pointers can be directly translated into raw Rust pointers. The C pointer `foo_t *` translates into a `*mut foo_t` in Rust and the C pointer `const foo_t *` translates to `*const foo_t` in Rust.

Opaque types are types that do not expose their contents. In C code, they are often written as `struct foo_t;` or `typedef struct foo_t foo_t;` - the types are given a name and no implementation in the public interface. Opaque types are only used behind pointers; you cannot construct an instance of the type yourself because you do not know what the implementation of the type looks like. We can achieve this by using an empty Rust enum:

```
pub enum image_t { }
pub enum row_t { }
```

Next up are structs. C structs are very similar to Rust structs, so translating them to Rust is fairly straightforward.

```
#[repr(C)]
pub struct header_t {
  pub width: libc::uint16_t,
  pub height: libc::uint16_t,
  pub format: Format
}

#[repr(C)]
pub struct block_t {
  pub data: *mut libc::c_char,
  pub width: libc::c_uint,
  pub height: libc::c_uint
}
```

In Rust, the compiler is allowed to reorder the fields of a struct to provide the most efficient layout of the struct. When interacting with foreign code, we must instruct the compiler to prevent that reordering by using the special #[repr(C)] attribute on the struct. That attribute is used to tell the compiler that you want a C-compatible layout for the struct.

C enums are similarly translated to Rust:

```
#[repr(C)]
pub enum Format {
  RGB8,
  RGBA8,
  PALETTE
}
```

Again, the #[repr(C)] attribute is used to indicate that the enum should be represented the same way it would be in C. We changed the name of both the type and its variants. The specific name is not required to be identical and changing it helps us to provide a more Rust-like API later.

Finally, typedefs are translated into Rust type aliases.

```
type modify_callback_t =
    extern "C" fn(*mut block_t,
                  *mut libc::c_void);
```

Since we are creating an alias to a C function type, we need to make sure that we translate the function type correctly. The important part here is the extern "C" part that indicates that this uses the C calling convention, not the Rust calling convention.

## C Type with no safe equivalent

We mentioned four cases where we can convert from a C type into an equivalent Rust type: opaque types, structs, enums, and typedefs. There is actually a fifth type that has no safe equivalent in Rust – the C union type. As of Rust 1.19, you can declare a union type in Rust like:

```
#[repr(C)]
union UnionType {
  f1: u8,
  f2: u32,
  f3: f32,
}
```

The union type in C is laid out with each field in the union overlaid onto the same memory. So, in the example, UnionType is large enough to hold the greatest of a u8, a u32, and a f32 (or, simply, a 32-bit wide memory location). At any one time, only one representation of the union is valid. This is similar to the Rust enum type, but the C union type does not carry any type information along with it, so the Rust union type has no way of encoding which variant is valid at any given time. That must be provided external to the type.

Since the compiler has no way of enforcing that the correct interpretation of the union has been used, reading the contents of the union is necessarily an unsafe operation. We can operate on C unions as follows:

```
let u = UnionType { f2: 42 };
let value = unsafe { u.f2 };
```

We create instances of the union similar to how we create an instance of a struct except that we can only specify one of the fields (since they all share the same storage). Again, accessing the contents of the field of a union must be wrapped in unsafe.

## Binding Functions

Now that we have our types, we can start binding the functions themselves. Binding to foreign functions is done using an **extern** block.

```
extern "C" {
  pub fn read_from_file(
    name: *const libc::c_char) -> *mut image_t;
  pub fn read_from_memory(
    data: *const libc::c_char,
    len: libc::c_uint) -> *mut image_t;

  pub fn destroy_image(image: *mut image_t);

  pub fn get_header(image: *const image_t,
                    header: *mut header_t);

  pub fn modify_image(image: *mut image_t,
                      block_width: libc::c_uint,
                      block_height: libc::c_uint,
                      cb: modify_callback_t,
                      user: *mut libc::c_void);

  pub fn first_row(
    image: *const image_t) -> *const row_t;
  pub fn next_row(
    row: *const row_t) -> *const row_t;
  pub fn row_data(
    row: *const row_t) -> *const libc::c_char;
}
```

Other than being in an **extern** block, binding to foreign functions is similar to defining regular Rust functions, just without a body. Binding to foreign functions is also similar to the declaration of a function in a header file in C. Making sure that the functions match the original C functions is important, as there is no way to check them automatically.

## Automatically Generating Bindings

If you have a large library that you are trying to wrap, then manually generating all of the foreign bindings can be tedious. Luckily, there does exist a crate on **crates.io** that can assist you with creating bindings for types and functions in C and C++ libraries. If you install the **bindgen** crate using:

```
cargo install bindgen
```

Then, you can run the following command to automatically generate bindings:

```
bindgen header.h -o bindings.rs
```

The bindgen utility walks through the passed-in header file, extracting all of the type definitions and function declarations from the header file. Then, it produces equivalent foreign function bindings inside of the output file. This can save you a lot of time if you want to use an entire library, but may be overkill if you only need to bind one or two functions.

## Wrapping the Library

With the Rust bindings to the foreign code in place, we should provide a safe wrapper for the library. Rust allows us to enforce conditions, such as ownership semantics, that the original library cannot, so we should look at the assumptions and restrictions the documentation for the C interface states when we are designing the wrapper.

### Wrapping image_t

The simplest types to wrap are the ones with ownership semantics that match Rust's. For our library, this is the image_t type, so we will quickly create a wrapper for image_t called Image.

```
struct Image {
  image: *mut image_t
}

impl Drop for Image {
  fn drop(&mut self) {
    unsafe {
      destroy_image(self.image);
    }
  }
}
```

The wrapper type contains an opaque pointer to an image_t. Now, the underlying library provides a function called destroy_image that should be called when the user is finished with the image. Luckily, Rust has a convenient way of determining when the user is finished with a value: a user is finished with a value when the value becomes inaccessible, though, being overwritten or going out of scope. Rust provides us with a trait to implement, called Drop, that has a method called drop that is called on any value when it becomes inaccessible. We can implement the Drop trait on the Image type to automatically call destroy_image when the Image is cleaned up.

Also, note the usage of unsafe around the call to destroy_image. All calls to foreign functions are implicitly unsafe, so we have to mark them as such. With our wrapper types, we are limiting the scope of the unsafe calls and making it so that users of our wrapper do not have to declare their code as unsafe.

Since we are here, we will also implement a couple of utility methods for constructing an Image.

```
use std::path::Path;
use std::ffi::CString;

impl Image {
  fn open<P: AsRef<Path>>(file: P)
    -> Option<Image> {
    let file = file.as_ref();
    let name = file.to_str().unwrap();
    let c_name = CString::new(name).unwrap();

    unsafe {
      let img_ptr = read_from_file(
          c_name.as_ptr());

      if img_ptr.is_null() {
        None
      } else {
        Some(Image {
          image: img_ptr
        })
      }
    }
  }
  fn from_bytes(bytes: &[u8]) -> Option<Image> {
    let ptr = bytes.as_ptr() as *const libc::c_char;
    let len = bytes.len() as libc::c_uint;

    unsafe {
      let img_ptr = read_from_memory(ptr, len);
      if img_ptr.is_null() {
        None
      } else {
```

```
        Some(Image {
          image: img_ptr
        })
      }
    }
  }
}
```

In the first function, we make use of several Rust features to present a usable API. First, the function is generic, taking any type that implements the `AsRef<Path>` trait. `AsRef` is a conversion trait that indicates that you can create a reference to another type. Several types implement `AsRef<Path>`, notably `&str`, `&Path` and `PathBuf`. This means our open method can take both a string and a path object constructed some other way.

The function we are wrapping, `read_from_file`, takes a single argument of type `*const c_char`. While the function's comment does not say explicitly, this normally indicates that it expects a null-terminated C string. Rust strings are not null-terminated, so we need to use the handy `CString` type from the standard library to help. First, we need to obtain a value that we can pass to `CString::new`, the easiest one here is a `&str`, which we can get by calling `to_str` on the `&Path` we create from the argument. `to_str` returns an `Option<&str>`, so we unwrap it to get at the underlying `&str`. Note that, if this was not example code, we would recommend returning a Result type and carrying out appropriate error-checking in this function instead of calling the unwraps, but for brevity, we will assume success. Finally, we construct the `CString` and use the `as_ptr` method to call `read_from_file`.

Finally, we check the return value of `read_from_file`. Since it can return null, we check for that return `None` if it is, and `Some(Image)` otherwise.

The second method is much simpler. We take a `&[u8]`, which is the best type for representing a chunk of raw data. The function then extracts the length and the pointer from the slice, and passes them to `read_from_memory`. We have to cast the raw `*const u8` pointer to a `*const c_char` pointer to match the signature of `read_from_memory`.

With only these few functions defined, our wrapper library is becoming safer and more Rust-like to use. We can load new images from disk or from memory and we can clean up after we are finished using them. Now, we just need to be able to manipulate the images.

## Constructing a Header

A common C pattern is found in the `get_header` function – passing a pointer to a structure that the function then writes into. In C, usage of the function would look like this:

```
header_t header;
get_header(image, &header);
```

However, trying to do the equivalent in Rust:

```
let mut header: header_t;
get_header(image, &mut header);
```

results in an error – `the use of a possibly uninitialized variable 'header'`. The fix is to initialize the variable before passing it to the function. Here are three common ways of doing so:

```
use std::mem;
pub struct Header(header_t);
impl Image {
  pub fn header1(&self) -> Header {
    let mut header = header_t {
      width: 0,
      height: 0,
      format: Format::RGB8
    }

    unsafe {
      get_header(self.image, &mut header);
    }

    Header(header)
  }
  pub fn header2(&self) -> Header {
    unsafe {
      let mut header: header_t = mem::zeroed();
      get_header(self.image, &mut header);
      Header(header)
    }
  }
  pub fn header3(&self) -> Header {
    unsafe {
      let mut header: header_t =
        mem::uninitialized();
      get_header(self.image, &mut header);
      Header(header)
    }
```

```
  }
}
```

header1 is the simplest solution. It initializes the struct with dummy values. This has the advantage of using the smallest amount of unsafe code, but might be unwieldy with larger structs. header2 and header3 instead use the mem::zeroed and mem::uninitialized functions, respectively. Both create a value of any type; mem::zeroed fills the entire value with zeroes, whereas mem::uninitialized leaves the value uninitialized.

Both mem::zeroed and mem::uninitialized are unsafe because there is no guarantee that "all zeroes" is valid for the type, and reading uninitialized data is never safe. That being said, if the function you are calling is not doing anything with the struct other than filling it in, both functions can be useful if performance is critical, as constructing a value has some cost.

## Wrapping header_t

We wrote the Header wrapper type above with the wrapped header_t as private. However, we would like users to be able to get at the data it contains. We will do this with some methods:

```
pub struct Header(header_t);
impl Header {
  #[inline(always)]
  pub fn width(&self) -> u16 {
    self.0.width
  }

  #[inline(always)]
  pub fn height(&self) -> u16 {
    self.0.height
  }

  #[inline(always)]
  pub fn format(&self) -> Format {
    self.0.format
  }
}
```

We have three fields and three methods. Notice that each one has the attribute #[inline(always)]; this tells the compiler to always inline the function. Simple accessor methods benefit greatly from inlining, so providing hints is recommended for them.

## Closures and Callbacks

The next thing to wrap is the modify_image function. It is a relatively complex function, so let us take another look at it.

```
type modify_callback_t =
    extern "C" fn(*mut block_t,
                  *mut libc::c_void) -> libc::c_int;

pub fn modify_image(image: *mut image_t,
                    block_width: libc::c_uint,
                    block_height: libc::c_uint,
                    cb: modify_callback_t,
                    user: *mut libc::c_void);
```

This function uses a relatively common callback pattern. In Rust, this is best translated as a closure. However, we cannot simply pass a closure into a C function – C does not know anything about Rust closures and would not know what to do with it. Instead, we need to do some work first.

Let us start with the method we are adding to Image:

```
pub struct Block(block_t);
impl Image {
  pub fn modify<F>(&mut self,
                   block_width: u32,
                   block_height: u32,
                   callback: F)
    where F: FnMut(&mut Block)
  {
    /***/
  }
}
```

This method roughly matches the modify_image function we are wrapping, except that instead of taking a function pointer and an opaque void *, we take a closure. This hints at how closures work and how we will take advantage of that.

We will cover the details of closures in another chapter. Here we will focus on just two aspects:

1. Closures are, logically, a combination of an "environment" and a function. When a closure is called, the function is passed into an extra

argument containing the environment, along with the arguments supplied when the closure is called.

2. Unboxed closures have a unique type. An unboxed closure is simply any closure that is not behind a pointer.

With this in mind, we can start to fill the body of `modify`:

```
use std::mem;
pub fn modify<F>(&mut self,
              block_width: u32,
              block_height: u32,
              mut callback: F)
  where F: FnMut(&mut Block)
{
  let user = &mut callback as *mut F
                           as *mut libc::c_void;
  let callback = wrapper::<F>;

  unsafe {
    modify_image(self.image,
                 block_width as libc::c_uint,
                 block_height as libc::c_uint,
                 callback, user);
  }

  extern "C" fn wrapper<F>(block: *mut block_t,
                           user: *mut libc::c_void)
    where F: FnMut(&mut Block)
  {
    unsafe {
      let callback = &mut *(user as *mut F);
      let block: &mut Block =
          mem::transmute(block);

      callback(block);
    }
  }
}
```

There is a fair bit happening here, so let us break it down, starting with the first few lines:

```
let user = &mut callback as *mut F
                         as *mut libc::c_void;
let callback = wrapper::<F>;
```

These lines are setting up the wrapper for the closure. We turn the closure passed to us into the `*mut libc::c_void` user argument: the rules around pointer casting require us to do the cast in two steps, first from `&mut F` to `*mut F`, then from `*mut F` to `*mut c_void`.

`callback` is more interesting – we set it to `wrapper::<F>`. `wrapper` is a generic function, so we have to provide the type it is generic over explicitly. `wrapper::<F>` gives us the function pointer we need to pass to `modify_image`.

The next line is just the call to `modify_image`, so we will skip that and move the most important part, the `wrapper` function. As mentioned before, it is a generic function that we pass to `modify_image`. Note the `extern "C"` in the definition which indicates that the function uses the C calling convention instead of the Rust one. Using the C calling convention is required as that is what the C code is expecting.

The first interesting line in the `wrapper` is this:

```
let callback = &mut *(user as *mut F);
```

This line is reconstructing the `&mut F` we had before from the `*mut c_void` pointer that was passed through the call to `modify_image` and then passed to `wrapper`.

Next up is this line:

```
let block: &mut Block = mem::transmute(block);
```

`transmute` is a special function that will convert between any two types that are the same size. `transmute` will be discussed in more detail later. For now, just know that this converts the `*mut block_t` that the `wrapper` function gets and turns it into a `&mut Block` we can pass to `callback`. The reason we construct it this way is to ensure that the `*mut block_t` and the `&mut Block` reference the same location. This is one of the few times where a `transmute` is necessary.

Finally, we have:

```
callback(block);
```

which calls the callback the user originally passed to the method, achieving the ultimate goal.

This pattern is very useful but has one strict requirement: the foreign function must pass a "user pointer" through from the function itself to the callback. This is often a void pointer, as in this case, but may be inside another structure.

## Using FnOnce

Your situation may be better served by using an `FnOnce` closure instead of an `FnMut` one. `FnOnce` closures can only be called once, which is good if you are only calling them once. However, simply replacing `FnMut` with `FnOnce` will result in this error:

```
error: cannot move out of borrowed content
```

This is because calling an `FnOnce` closure moves it, preventing further calls. The way to adapt the pattern is this:

```
use std::mem;
pub fn modify_once<F>(&mut self,
                      block_width: u32,
                      block_height: u32,
                      callback: F)
  where F: FnOnce(&mut Block)
{
  let mut callback = Some(callback);
  let user = &mut callback as *mut Option<F>
                           as *mut libc::c_void;
  let callback = wrapper::<F>;

  unsafe {
    modify_image(self.image,
                 block_width as libc::c_uint,
                 block_height as libc::c_uint,
                 callback, user);
  }

  extern "C" fn wrapper<F>(block: *mut block_t,
                           user: *mut libc::c_void)
    where F: FnOnce(&mut Block)
  {
    unsafe {
      let callback = &mut *(user as *mut Option<F>);
      let callback = callback.take().unwrap();
      let block : &mut Block =
          mem::transmute(block);
```

```
            callback(block);
        }
      }
    }
```

The lines of interest here are highlighted. What we are doing here is creating an &mut Option<F> instead of an &mut F and using that as the user pointer. In the wrapper, instead of calling the callback directly, we extract the closure from the &mut Option<F>, replacing it with None. take still returns an Option<F> though, so we unwrap the Option and call the result of that.

The reason for the Option dance is to make sure that all data is cleaned up correctly. In the modify_once method, the value in the callback variable is Some(closure) before the call to the modify_once foreign function. After the call, the value in callback is None, since the wrapper stores None as part of extracting the closure. This prevents the closure itself from being cleaned up at the end of the method, mimicking the behavior you would see if you passed the closure by-value.

## Wrapping an Iterator

```
pub fn first_row(
  image: *const image_t) -> *const row_t;
pub fn next_row(
  row: *const row_t) -> *const row_t;
pub fn row_data(
  row: *const row_t) -> *const libc::c_char;
```

The last three functions allow you to iterate over the rows in the image. The natural way to wrap these is in a Rust iterator. The comments in the original header give us some lifetime information we can express directly in Rust.

```
use std::slice;
pub struct Rows<'a> {
  image: &'a Image,
  current_row: *const row_t
}
impl<'a> Iterator for Rows<'a> {
  type Item = Vec<u8>;

  fn next(&mut self) -> Option<Vec<u8>> {
    if self.current_row.is_null() {
      return None;
```

```
    }

    unsafe {
      let data = row_data(self.current_row);
      let len = self.image.get_header().width();
      let slice = slice::from_raw_parts(
        data as *const u8, len as usize);
      let vec = slice.to_owned();
      self.current_row = next_row(self.current_row);
      Some(vec)
    }
  }
}
impl Image {
  pub fn rows<'a>(&'a self) -> Rows<'a> {
    let row = unsafe { first_row(self.image) };
    Rows {
      image: self,
      current_row: row,
    }
  }
}
```

This is a fairly straightforward iterator. By storing a reference to `Image` in the iterator, we enforce the constraint that the `row_t` pointer will not be used after the image is destroyed, since the lifetime of the iterator is tied to the lifetime of the `Image`. In the body of the `next` method, we first construct a slice from the row data and the width of the image, then copy it to a `Vec<u8>` before advancing to the next row. This is necessary because calling `next_row` will invalidate the previous pointer from `row_data`.

This iterator works, but has some flaws. The biggest one is that it must copy the data for each row in order to be safe. We could avoid the copy if we could express that you cannot call next while the previous row is still around. Fortunately, we have a pattern just for this case – streaming iterators. The C API is much better suited to a streaming iterator pattern, so let us do that instead.

```
use std::slice;
pub struct Rows<'a> {
  image: &'a Image,
  current_row: *const row_t,
  first: bool
}
impl<'a> Rows<'a> {
  pub fn next<'b>(&'b mut self)
```

```
      -> Option<&'b [u8]> {
      if !self.first {
        unsafe {
           self.current_row = next_row(self.current_row);
        }
      }
      self.first = false;
      if self.current_row.is_null() {
        return None;
      }

      unsafe {
        let data = row_data(self.current_row);
        let len = self.image.get_header().width();
        let slice = slice::from_raw_parts(
          data as *const u8, len as usize);
        Some(slice)
      }
    }
  }
  impl Image {
    pub fn rows<'a>(&'a self) -> Rows<'a> {
      let row = unsafe { first_row(self.image) };
      Rows {
        image: self,
        current_row: row,
        first: true
      }
    }
  }
```

The streaming iterator version is very similar to the regular iterator, with a few key differences. The most obvious one is the additional `first` field added to the iterator itself. This is because we have to advance to the next row before getting the data for that row, but also to return the data for the first row. The other difference is that the streaming iterator produces slices, not `Vec<u8>`s, which is much more efficient, as it no longer copies all the data each iteration.

## EXPOSING RUST

Being able to use foreign functions in Rust is great, but what if you want to call Rust code from another language? Fortunately, Rust is just as capable of doing that as it is at using foreign code.

Many other languages support using foreign code via a native interface that works with C functions. Rust can expose functions that look like C functions, allowing those language to talk to your Rust code.

As with the previous section, we will need some code to write an interface for. We have a simple audio decoding library to work with. The implementation details have been omitted.

```
use std::io::Read;

pub struct AudioStream<R: ?Sized> {
    stream: R,
}

impl<R: Read> AudioStream<R> {
    pub fn new(stream: R) -> AudioStream<R> {
        AudioStream { stream: stream }
    }
}

impl<R: ?Sized + Read> AudioStream<R> {
    pub fn samples<'a>(&'a mut self) -> Samples<'a, R> {
        Samples::new(self)
    }
}

pub struct Samples<'a, R: 'a + Read + ?Sized> {
    stream: &'a mut AudioStream<R>,
}

impl<'a, R: 'a + Read + ?Sized> Samples<'a, R> {
    pub fn new(stream: &'a mut AudioStream<R>) -> Samples<'a, R> {
        Samples {
            stream: stream
        }
    }
}

impl<'a, R: 'a + Read + ?Sized> Iterator for Samples<'a, R> {
    type Item = f32;

    fn next(&mut self) -> Option<f32> {
        unimplemented!();
    }
}
```

## Wrapping AudioStream

First off, let us look at wrapping the AudioStream type. It is a fairly typical Rust type for working with I/O. It is generic over all types that implement the Read trait, allowing it to work with a variety of input types. C, however, does not have generics so we will need to expose the type in such a way that it does not require generic typing.

```
use libc::{c_char, size_t};
use std::ffi::CStr;
use std::fs::File;
use std::io::Cursor;
use std::ptr;
use std::slice;

type audiostream_t = Box<AudioStream<Read>>;

fn make_audiostream<R: Read+'static>(
  stream: R) -> *mut audiostream_t {
  let stream = AudioStream::new(stream);
  let stream: Box<AudioStream<Read>> =
    Box::new(stream);
  let stream = Box::new(stream);
  Box::into_raw(stream)
}

#[no_mangle]
pub extern "C" fn rs_audiostream_from_ptr(
  p: *const u8, len: size_t) -> *mut audiostream_t {
  if p.is_null() { return ptr::null_mut(); }
  let bytes = unsafe { slice::from_raw_parts(
    p, len as usize) };
  let bytes: Vec<u8> = bytes.to_owned();
  let bytes = Cursor::new(bytes);

  make_audiostream(bytes)
}
```

The first interesting line is this one:

```
type audiostream_t = Box<AudioStream<Read>>;
```

It defines the type we will be returning pointers to as part of the API. The type we are using is actually trait object type. While you may have seen trait objects like Box<Error>, this is a more advanced case where the trait is embedded into a struct. The important thing is that it gets rid of, or "erases", the specific Read type we used to construct the stream.

Next up is the make_audiostream function. This is a helper function that takes an input and returns a raw pointer to an audiostream_t. The interesting line in the function is this one:

```
Box::into_raw(stream)
```

It turns our Box<audiostream_t> into a *mut audiostream_t. This function handles the conversion from Box<T> to *mut T, making sure that the Box is not freed early. It is strongly recommended that you use this function instead of manually constructing the appropriate pointer yourself.

Finally, we have a function for constructing an audio stream from a block of memory. There are a number of important things going on with this function, but let us start with the signature:

```
pub extern "C" fn rs_audiostream_from_ptr(
  p: *const u8, len: size_t) -> *mut audiostream_t
```

There exists a lot of similarity to how we defined foreign functions in the earlier section. The most significant part is the extern "C". As we saw before, this indicates that it uses the C calling convention instead of the Rust one. Next, we will take a look at the attribute

```
#[no_mangle]
```

This attribute is very important for the wrapper. It tells the compiler to not mangle the symbol names it puts into the library. Since the library formats in common use do not understand concepts like modules and generics, the Rust compiler has to prevent duplicate symbols in the library by encoding module and type information into the name, or "mangling" the name. Without the attribute, the symbol placed into the library would look a little like this:

```
_ZN7rsaudio23rs_audiostream_from_ptr17h274a34aa5cf68027E
```

While this is a valid symbol name that Rust understands, a C program is not going to understand that these are the same symbols as rs_audiostream_from_ptr. The no_mangle attribute tells the compiler to use the name we gave it, so the function will be named as `rs_audiostream_from_ptr` instead.

The body of the function constructs a `Vec<u8>` from the given pointer and wraps it in a `Cursor` to provide a `Read` interface for the data. The `Cursor` is then used to construct the audio stream. We copy the data given because we cannot ensure that the pointer we are passed will live long enough.

Finally, let us write another construction function that takes a filename for the library to open.

```
#[no_mangle]
pub extern "C" fn rs_audiostream_from_file(file: *const c_char) ->
                    *mut audiostream_t {
  if file.is_null() { return ptr::null_mut(); }
  let file = unsafe { CStr::from_ptr(file) };
  let file = if let Ok(f) = file.to_str() {
    f
  } else {
    return ptr::null_mut();
  };

  let file = if let Ok(f) = File::open(file) {
    f
  } else {
    return ptr::null_mut();
  };

  make_audiostream(file)
}
```

The bulk of this function is actually error-handling. It is common in C to indicate failure using the return type. In this case, we use a null pointer to indicate failure. Other than the error handling, the function first constructs a `&CStr` from the given pointer, then turns it into a `&str` which it uses to open a file and finally, construct an audio stream.

The last part of the wrapper is the destroy function, which will clean up the code:

```
#[no_mangle]
pub extern "C" fn rs_destroy_audiostream(stream: *mut audiostream_t) {
```

```
    unsafe {
      let _stream = Box::from_raw(stream);
    }
  }
```

All this function does is turn the raw `*mut audiostream_t` pointer back into a `Box<audiostream_t>` and let it be dropped at the end of the scope. This will also handle the cleanup of the contained input stream.

## Wrapping Samples

Wrapping an iterator requires exposing the Iterator protocol in a more explicit way. Iterators use a `next` method that returns a `Option`; if `next` returns `None`, then the iterator is finished. Translating this to C requires some care, however. While in Rust we can use the `Option` type to have a universal `None` value, such a thing does not exist in C. Instead, we need to come up with a way of indicating "end of iteration" in some other way.

```
type samples_t = Samples<'static, Read>;

#[no_mangle]
pub extern "C" fn rs_new_samples(stream: *mut audiostream_t) ->
        *mut samples_t {if stream.is_null() { return ptr::null_mut(); }
  let stream = unsafe { &mut *stream };

  let samples = stream.samples();
  let samples = Box::new(samples);
  let samples = Box::into_raw(samples);

  samples as *mut samples_t
}

#[no_mangle]
pub extern "C" fn rs_destroy_samples(samples: *mut samples_t) {
  unsafe {
    let _samples = Box::from_raw(samples);
  }
}
#[no_mangle]
pub extern "C" fn rs_samples_next(
  samples: *mut samples_t,
```

```
  sample: *mut f32) -> i32 {
  if samples.is_null() { return 1; }
  let samples = unsafe { &mut *samples };
  if let Some(s) = samples.next() {
    unsafe { *sample = s; }
    return 0;
  } else {
    return 1;
  }
}
```

The first two functions are construction and cleanup functions for the iterator. Like the AudioStream wrapper earlier, we are using Box to create a pointer that we can return from the function. The function we are interested in is the third one: `rs_samples_next`.

The signature of `rs_samples_next` might be difficult to see in the above code, so let us compress it a bit.

```
fn(*mut samples_t, *mut f32) -> i32
```

The function takes two pointers, one is a pointer to the iterator, the other is a pointer to an `f32`. It also returns an `i32`. The pattern we are using is relatively common in C code; the return value is an indicator for success while the value we care about is written into the given pointer. To demonstrate, here is an example of it being used in a C function:

```
void print_samples(samples_t *samples) {
  float sample;

  while (!rs_samples_next(samples, &sample)) {
    printf("%f\n", sample);
  }
}
```

It loops over all the samples and prints each value. `rs_samples_next` returns 1 when iteration is finished and 0 otherwise, so `!rs_samples_next(samples, &sample)` will be true when `rs_samples_next` returns 0, and false otherwise.

As you can see, exposing a foreign API around safe Rust code is fairly straightforward.

## KEY TAKEAWAYS

- Rust's foreign function interface allows Rust code to easily reuse existing native system libraries by exposing an unsafe view of the foreign functions and types.
- Typically, you should create a safe, higher-level Rust API on top of the low-level foreign API that you consume with the foreign function interface.
- Rust also allows you to go the other way. You can create a library in Rust using safe code and then expose a thin foreign interface around that safe code for foreign languages to use.

# 12

# Interior Mutability

One of Rust's greatest strengths is its type system. The language goes to great lengths to enforce safety at compile-time, preventing a large set of bugs from ever occurring. Sometimes, though, a compile-time check may not be enough. There are times when you know that the code you are constructing is correct, but the static checks that Rust provides may disagree. That is the nature of static analysis; it cannot take into account how programming constructs are actually used at run-time – it only determines what it is possible for the program to do. Fortunately, Rust comes with an escape hatch in the form of unsafe code to allow you to ease back on some of the restrictions (such as the restrictions on aliasing mutable variables) that Rust normally enforces for safe code

Before we dive into unsafe code, however, we will take a look at a concept that allows you to safely circumvent the restrictions on aliasing mutable variables: Interior Mutability.

## WHAT AND WHY?

Interior mutability refers to the ability to mutate data behind an immutable reference. Recall that mutability is normally "inherited"; a value inside a mutable variable is itself mutable. Interior mutability breaks this by allowing you to mutate data, regardless of inherited mutability.

Interior mutability is required because Rust possesses limited information when checking programs. It has to assume the worst and that causes otherwise valid programs to be rejected. For example:

```
struct Foo {
  value: Option<i32>
}

impl Foo {
  fn get_value(&self) -> i32 {
    self.value.unwrap_or(-1)
  }

  fn set_value(&self, v: Option<i32>) {
    self.value = v;
  }
}
```

Rust will produce a compile-time error in `set_value`, complaining about assigning to an immutable borrow. While the code, as written, seems safe at first glance, it is important to remember that Rust only looks at a single function at a time. Even if the following function does not exist, Rust must assume it might.

```
  fn something_silly(&self) {
    match self.value {
      Some(ref v) => {
        self.set_value(None);
        println!("{}", v);
      }
      _ => ()
    }
  }
```

Here, it becomes clear why Rust must reject the original code – we take a reference to the `i32` in the `Option<i32>`, only to overwrite the field. The reference now points to a location that could be anything. While the problems here are limited, a more complex example might cause a segmentation fault (the program crashing), or worse, silent memory corruption.

Interior mutability allows you to write through an immutable reference, on the promise that you will not break the rules normally used. Fortunately, the standard library contains two types that provide interior mutability safely: `Cell` and `RefCell`.

# CELL AND REFCELL

`Cell` and `RefCell` provide safe access to interior mutability by enforcing the rules in different ways. We will take a look at `Cell` first.

## Cell

There are two important things to note about `Cell`:

1. The `Cell` type only allows you to 'get' types that implement `Copy`; otherwise, you must take ownership of the value using `into_inner`.
2. The `Cell` type only gives and accepts values for reading and writing, not references.

These two factors are what allow `Cell` to be safely mutated through an immutable reference.

```
pub struct Cell<T> { /***/ }

impl<T: Copy> Cell<T> {
  pub fn get(&self) -> T { /***/ }
}
impl Cell<T> {
  pub fn set(&self, value: T) { /***/ }
}
```

In the previous section, we saw how Rust will reject a program because the compiler has to assume that there might be a reference elsewhere and that mutation could invalidate that reference. `Cell` works around this issue by not allowing you to ever get a reference to its contents. Thus, there is never a reference to invalidate.

`Cell` requires `Copy` so it can return a value from the `get` method. If the type was one that moved, the `Cell` would have to be destroyed when getting the value, which somewhat limits its usefulness. `Cell` does not require `Clone` because `Clone` takes a reference to `self` and the safety of `Cell` is dependent on code not having a reference to the value stored in the `Cell`.

Altering our earlier example to use `Cell` looks like this:

```
use std::cell::Cell;
struct Foo {
  value: Cell<Option<i32>>
}

impl Foo {
  fn get_value(&self) -> i32 {
    self.value.get().unwrap_or(-1)
  }

  fn set_value(&self, v: Option<i32>) {
    self.value.set(v);
  }
}
```

We cannot write the `something_silly` function, because that function would require us to be able to get a reference to the value. At compile-time, `Cell` enforces that a reference to the interior value cannot exist. But what if we still needed to be able to get a reference to the interior value, though, and promised that we would never write a function that violated the rules?

## RefCell

Where `Cell` enforces Rust's rules by making it impossible to break them, `RefCell` enforces the rules by checking them at run-time and throwing an error if you break them.

```
pub struct RefCell<T> { /***/ }

impl<T> RefCell<T> {
  fn borrow(&self) -> Ref<T> { /***/ }

  fn borrow_mut(&self) -> RefMut<T> {
    /***/
  }
  fn try_borrow(&self) -> Result<Ref<T>, BorrowError> { /***/ }

  fn try_borrow_mut(&self) -> Result<RefMut<T>, BorrowMutError> {
    /***/
  }
}
```

`RefCell` records how many immutable references it has given out, and whether or not it has given out a mutable reference at run-time, panicking if you try to get an immutable reference while a mutable one already exists, or a mutable reference while any reference already exists. You can use the `try_borrow` and `try_borrow_mut` functions to return an error instead of panicking.

`RefCell` can be used like this:

```
struct Foo {
  cache: RefCell<HashMap<i32, i32>>
}

impl Foo {
  fn get_value(&self, key: i32) -> i32 {
    let mut cache = self.cache.borrow_mut();
    *cache.entry(key).or_insert_with(|| {
      do_expensive_calculation(key)
    })
  }
}
```

Here, we are using a `HashMap` to cache the result of a calculation. If the `key` is already in the map, we return the associated value; otherwise, we calculate the value, store it in the map, and then return it.

## WHERE TO USE INTERIOR MUTABILITY

Interior mutability is a way around Rust's compile-time checking; therefore, it is important to only use it when Rust's checks prevent your code from working. As much as possible, programs should be structured so that interior mutability is not required, taking advantage of the guarantees of the language instead.

The main rule to adhere to when utilizing interior mutability is this:

> Do not return references to the data you are mutating.

This rule is enforced by both `Cell` (as you cannot take a reference to its contents) and `RefCell` (via lifetime rules); however, it is important to keep it in mind when evaluating whether or not interior mutability will work for you. To understand why this rule is in place, we need to take another look at references.

## Immutable & Mutable vs. Shared & Unique

In previous chapters, we called `&T` an "immutable reference" and `&mut T` a "mutable reference". This is a useful way to consider them as often as you either need mutability or not and the restrictions on the references are something you have to deal with. However, a more accurate view of references is to consider `&T` aa a "shared reference" and `&mut T` as a "unique reference". The ability to mutate or not using the reference is instead tied to whether or not we know that the reference is the only one. `&T` is immutable because it is a shared reference and `&mut T` is mutable because it is unique.

This view of references is what `RefCell` is enforcing at runtime. Part of this enforcement, however, limits what you can do with the references `RefCell` gives you. The rule to use is whether or not your code could break the uniqueness rule.

```
struct Foo {
  val: RefCell<Vec<i32>>
}

impl Foo {
  fn get_val(&self) -> &mut Vec<i32> { /***/ }
}
```

This code could break the uniqueness rule. Since immutable references can be shared, two different pieces of code can have the same `&Foo` reference. Since `get_val` can be called on a `&Foo` reference, this means that `get_val` could be called on each of them, producing the same `&mut Vec<i32>` reference and violating the uniqueness rule. `RefCell` will prevent this at runtime by panicking, but it is useful to know that the pattern will not work before you try.

With this in mind, there are two common scenarios for which interior mutability makes sense: logical immutability and the efficient use of references.

## Logical Immutability

This pattern is one we have already seen – a memoization cache is an instance of the "logical immutability" pattern. Here, the interior mutability is just an implementation detail and not exposed to the user. If the cache did not exist, the end user would see exactly the same value produced by get_value for each key given as an argument. Logically, the Foo struct is immutable because the fact that we are putting the value in the cache does not affect the outcome of the functions operating on the Foo struct.

```
struct Foo {
  cache: RefCell<HashMap<i32, i32>>
}

impl Foo {
  fn get_value(&self, key: i32) -> i32 {
    let mut cache = self.cache.borrow_mut();
    *cache.entry(key).or_insert_with(|| {
      do_expensive_calculation(key)
    })
  }
}
```

Another application of logical immutability is for "side-channel" functionality. Side-channel functionality occurs when you want to do some mutation in a method that is really immutable, such as tracking call statistics in a program.

```
pub struct Foo {
  bar: Bar,
  foo_count: Cell<usize>
}
impl Foo {
  pub fn do_foo<'a>(&'a self) -> &'a Bar {
    self.do_foo_called();
    &self.bar
  }

  fn do_foo_called(&self) {
    let prev = self.foo_count.get();
    self.foo_count.set(prev + 1);
  }
}
```

This is especially useful when the functionality you need mutation for is intended for internal use only, such as debugging, which prevents those internal details from leaking into the public API.

## Efficient Use of References

One advantage of using references is that there is very little cost to reading from them. As such, it is generally a good idea to try to return references to data instead of copying it as much as possible. The issue arises when you also want to mutate data that is contained in the same type you got the reference from.

```
struct Level {
  enemies: Vec<Enemy>,
  selected_enemy: Cell<EnemyId>
}

impl Level {
  fn enemies<'a>(&'a self) -> &'a [Enemy] {
    &self.enemies[..]
  }

  fn set_selected_enemy(&self, id: EnemyId) {
    self.selected_enemy.set(id);
  }

  fn selected_enemy<'a>(
    &'a self) -> Option<&'a Enemy> {
    /* Find enemy using selected_enemy */
  }
}

fn do_game() {
  let level = Level::new();
  /***/

  for enemy in level.enemies() {
    if under_cursor(cursor_position, enemy) {
      level.set_selected_enemy(enemy.id);
      break;
    }
  }

  /***/
}
```

In this code, getting the list of enemies in the level borrows the level itself. Without interior mutability, we would be prevented from modifying the `selected_enemy` field while iterating over the enemies.

This pattern is most useful when you have complex objects that should not, or cannot, be copied, but the uniqueness enforced by using a mutable reference is too restrictive. This is especially true when you start storing references in other types, as there may not be an obvious place to end the borrows so you can perform the mutation.

### UNSAFECELL

The last thing to discuss when it comes to interior mutability is `UnsafeCell`. `UnsafeCell` is a special type that indicates to the compiler that you are using interior mutability. It is used to implement both `Cell` and `RefCell` and is the only way to safely obtain a mutable reference from an immutable one.

`UnsafeCell` is not intended for regular use; you almost certainly want to use `Cell` or `RefCell` instead. `UnsafeCell` does not enforce any of the invariants the language requires. Instead, you have to do that yourself. In general, `UnsafeCell` is used behind the scenes to implement types like `Cell` and `RefCell`. If, however, you find yourself needing interior mutability but find that `Cell` and `RefCell` are too restrictive, and are confident that your design is safe, `UnsafeCell` can be a useful tool when working with unsafe Rust code. Just remember, the Rust compiler provides very few protections when working with this type!

## KEY TAKEAWAYS

- You can ease up on Rust's restrictions on unique, mutable, references by using interior mutability.
- `Cell` provides a way to mutate a field in a struct by allowing you to obtain or set values to the field.
- `RefCell` provides a way to take a mutable reference to a field in an otherwise immutable struct. `RefCell` enforces, at run-time, that only one mutable reference to the contents of the `RefCell` exist at any one time.

# 13

# Unsafe Rust

Rust describes itself as a "systems programming language", but what is "systems programming", how is it different to other types of programming, and what does it have to do with unsafe code? In this chapter, we will explain systems programming, why unsafe Rust is necessary because of it, and how to make the best use of Rust's features when working with unsafe code.

## SYSTEMS PROGRAMMING

Systems programming, as it is used here, refers to building software systems, as opposed to software applications. An application is software that the user directly interacts with, such as a word processor or video player. A system is software that provides services to other software, such as an operating system or game engine. Systems often have strict performance requirements.

It is not always easy to separate the "system" and the "application" aspects of some programs. A web browser is interacted with directly, but it also contains many systems within it. The rendering engine and the Javascript interpreter both fit within our system definition above. It is important to not restrict yourself to thinking that a program is either a system or an application and instead think of the system and application aspects of the program.

While systems can be written in any language, performance is often a priority. If performance is a high enough priority, any language that takes away control of computer resources from the programmer is unsuitable.

## Enter Rust

Even without unsafe code, Rust can be used for many systems programming tasks. It compiles to native code and gives precise control over computer memory and other resources. However, even this is not always enough. Rust's safety features sometimes prevent you from writing faster code, even when that code is safe. Lower performance may be acceptable, but when it is not, Unsafe Rust provides an "escape hatch".

Unsafe Rust allows you to use only a handful of extra features. In unsafe code, you can:

- dereference a raw pointer,
- call an unsafe or foreign function,
- implement unsafe traits,
- access the fields of unions, and
- read or write a mutable static variable.

Unsafe code is indicated by the use of the `unsafe` keyword, either in a function definition or as a block. The semantics of code marked as "unsafe" does not change, however. The same ownership, borrowing, and type rules still apply; the unsafe relaxation only allows access to the above named features.

### When to Use Unsafe

The use of `unsafe` discussed here does not include the unsafe used in the Foreign Function Interface chapter. The use of `unsafe` there was mostly to allow the calling of foreign functions, so the decision was made for us already.

Unsafe Rust allows access to a small number of features that provide an incredible amount of flexibility and power. The cost is that the safety of code using those features cannot be fully determined by the compiler, so the programmer has to make a greater effort to ensure the safety of the code. While you can be confident that code written only with Safe Rust is free of memory errors and other errors due to extensive static checking, unsafe code receives much less scrutiny by the compiler. It is on you, the programmer, to assess the correctness of unsafe code.

As such, using unsafe Rust should be carefully considered. Difficulties with Rust's type system and static checking often reflect flaws in the code's design. If a different design is not acceptable, or possible, then unsafe code may be appropriate.

Unsafe code is most commonly used for constructing data structures. The standard library makes heavy use of unsafe code for implementing `Vec<T>`, `HashMap<K, V>` and other common data structures. If you find yourself needing to implement a data structure and fighting the compiler on it, unsafe code is likely acceptable.

## Unsafe Code Best Practices

Writing unsafe code can be a daunting prospect. There are many ways to get it wrong, to break things, and generally cause havoc. The compiler is trusting you, the programmer, to have written correct code. Fortunately, there are some excellent practices to help you work with unsafe code.

### Keep Unsafe Code Small

To paraphrase C. A. R. Hoare, code can be simple enough that there are no obvious deficiencies, or so complex that there are no obvious deficiencies. The same idea applies to unsafe code in Rust.

Since you can no longer rely on the compiler to recognize your mistakes, you should keep unsafe code as small as possible so you can easily be sure of its correctness. Many of the following practices are aimed at reducing the overall size and scope of your unsafe code.

## Preserve Rust's Invariants

This is a strict requirement for unsafe code since breaking the invariants Rust has can lead to errors across your entire program. A full list of invariants to maintain is out of scope for this book; however, it is unlikely that you will break most of them by accident. The main ones you need to be aware of are these:

- Do not alias `&mut` pointers. One of the most important assumptions Rust makes is that two independent `&mut` pointers refer to different places. Since unsafe code allows you to construct `&mut` pointers from raw pointers, you must make sure that another `&mut` pointer to the same place is not constructed.
- Do not alias `&mut` pointers and `&` pointers. Similar to the previous invariant, Rust assumes that independent `&mut` and `&` pointers do not alias either.
- Correctly align pointers. All pointers in Rust, raw and otherwise, are assumed to be correctly aligned for the type they point to. This means that if you have a `*const u32`, the address stored in the pointer is aligned to a four-byte boundary. When converting between pointer types, you need to be aware of this invariant and make sure that your pointers are appropriately aligned.

## Create Abstractions for Unsafe Code

One of the great advantages of Rust is its type system. The type system allows you to enforce constraints at compile-time rather than relying on run-time checks or the user, following some rules. This advantage is especially great when working with unsafe code.

```
struct DList<T> {
  head: *mut Node<T>,
  tail: *mut Node<T>
}

struct Node<T> {
  prev: *mut Node<T>,
  next: *mut Node<T>,
  data: T
}
```

Above is the basic structure of a doubly-linked list. Each node has a pointer to the previous and subsequent nodes in the chain. This kind of structure inherently contains aliasing and, therefore, cannot be easily represented using safe code, so we use raw pointers instead. If there is no previous or subsequent node, the pointer is null.

A possible way to implement insertion into this list is as follows:

```
impl<T> Node<T> {
  fn insert_after(&mut self, node: *mut Node<T>) {
    unsafe {
      let next = self.next;
      self.next = node;
      (*node).prev = self;
      (*node).next = next;
      (*next).prev = node;
    }
  }
}
```

This code compiles, but contains a bug. Can you see it? We do not check to see if the `next` pointer is null. If the insertion point is at the end of the list, this code will crash.

What if we could force the null check? To do that, we want an omitted null-check to result in a compile-time error instead of a run-time one. `Option<T>` is the perfect tool for this job.

```
impl<T> Node<T> {
  fn next<'a>(&'a self) -> Option<&'a Node<T>> {
    if self.next.is_null() {
      None
    } else {
      unsafe { Some(&*self.next) }
    }
  }

  fn next_mut<'a>(&'a mut self) -> Option<&'a mut Node<T>> {
    if self.next.is_null() {
      None
    } else {
      unsafe { Some(&mut *self.next) }
    }
  }
```

```
    fn insert_after(&mut self, node: *mut Node<T>) {
      unsafe {
        (*node).prev = self;
        (*node).next = self.next;
        if let Some(next) = self.next_mut() {
          next.prev = node;
        }
        self.next = node;
      }
    }
  }
```

That's a little better. The helper functions return Option, requiring pattern matching to get at the contained pointer, if it exists. It is not as good as it could be, though. We can still use the raw pointers directly; there is no way to force use of the helper methods in this situation.

What if we abstracted away the raw pointers themselves?

```
  struct Link<T> {
    ptr: *mut Node<T>
  }

  impl<T> Clone for Link<T> {
    fn clone(&self) -> Link<T> {
      Link {
        ptr: self.ptr
      }
    }
  }

  impl<T> Link<T> {
    fn new(ptr: *mut Node<T>) -> Link<T> {
      Link { ptr: ptr }
    }

    fn get<'a>(&'a self) -> Option<&'a Node<T>> {
      if self.is_null() {
        None
      } else {
        unsafe { Some(&*self.ptr) }
      }
    }

    unsafe fn get_mut<'a>(&'a mut self) -> Option<&'a mut Node<T>> {
      if self.is_null() {
```

```
            None
        } else {
            Some(&mut *self.ptr)
        }
    }

    fn is_null(&self) -> bool {
        self.ptr.is_null()
    }
}
```

Here, we have created a `Link` type, which is a simple wrapper over the raw pointer from before. An important detail is that the `get_mut` method is marked as unsafe. This is because we cannot ensure that two independent `Link<T>`s will not actually point to the same place and therefore produce aliasing `&mut` pointers. By marking the method as `unsafe`, we push the responsibility up to the caller.

We also only provide a `Clone` implementation, not a `Copy` one. This helps avoid accidental aliasing, since copying the link must be done explicitly. Let us update `Node<T>` and `insert_after` to use `Link<T>`:

```
struct Node<T> {
    prev: Link<T>,
    next: Link<T>,
    data: T
}
impl<T> Node<T> {
    fn insert_after(&mut self, mut node: Link<T>) {
        unsafe {
            if let Some(node) = node.get_mut() {
                node.prev = Link::new(self);
                node.next = self.next.clone();
            } else {
                panic!("Cannot insert an empty node");
            }
            if let Some(next) = self.next.get_mut() {
                next.prev = node.clone();
            }
            self.next = node;
        }
    }
}
```

It looks similar to the previous version, except that we now also check that the passed-in pointer is also valid. The more important thing is that we have made it much more difficult to work directly with the raw pointers.

## Using Unsafe code for performance

There are several other places that we may want to use unsafe code for performance reasons. Consider the following code:

```
fn sum(slice: &[usize]) -> usize {
    let mut sum = 0;
    for x in 0..slice.len() {
        sum += slice[x];
    }
    sum
}
```

In the above example, we are using the indexing operator to get the value at the x index for each index in the loop. However, to be safe, the index operator performs bounds-checking to ensure that the index is within the bounds of the slice before returning a reference to the value found at that index, panicking if the index is out of bounds. Normally, this bounds check is not burdensome since it is very efficient. However, when you are trying to eke the most performance out of an inner loop of code, check the bounds of a slice every time you are indexing into it might be too heavy-weight. We can restructure our code slightly to take advantage of unsafe code to eliminate the bounds check.

```
fn sum(slice: &[usize]) -> usize {
    let mut sum = 0;
    for x in 0..slice.len() {
        sum += unsafe { *slice.get_unchecked(x) };
    }
    sum
}
```

In the above restructuring, we are taking advantage of an unsafe API call on slices that simply return a reference to the value in the slice. In the example, this is safe because we are assured that the index is in bounds since our loop only runs within the bounds of the slice. Effectively, we are performing the bounds check to ensure that we are still within the for loop, so there is no need to do so when we are accessing the slice.

Rust has several unsafe, "unchecked" methods on different data structures that eliminate some sort of safety checks such as bounds checking on indices. By convention, Rust suffixes these types of unsafe methods with `unchecked`. Here are several more examples of unchecked methods that you might find useful if you need some extra speed and are confident that data is formatted in such a way that the code is really safe:

- `CString::from_vec_unchecked(Vec<u8>)` – creates a C-style string directly by appending a `NULL` byte to the vector and without verifying that the vector contains no interior `NULL` bytes.
- `String::from_utf8_unchecked(Vec<u8>)` – creates a UTF-8 String without verifying that the string corresponds to valid UTF-8.
- `char::from_u32_unchecked(u32)` – creates a UTF-8 character from a `u32` without any verification.

## KEY TAKEAWAYS

- Unsafe code only allows you the extra abilities to dereference raw pointers, call unsafe or foreign functions, implement unsafe traits, access fields of unions, or read and write mutable static variables.
- It is important to still preserve Rust's invariants when working with unsafe code; otherwise, you cause errors to spread through the rest of your safe Rust program.
- The best way to work with unsafe code is to minimize the scope of unsafe by creating safe abstractions around it. Minimizing the scope allows you to carefully verify that your unsafe blocks are correct.

# Index

## Symbols



## A

## B



## C

## M

**N**



**O**



**P**

## Q



## R

## U